WORLD TO COME

THE RETURN OF TRUMP
AND THE END OF THE OLD ORDER

Mathew Burrows
&
Josef Braml

BRIXTON INK

Dr. Mathew Burrows is the Counselor and Program Lead of the Stimson Center's Strategic Foresight Hub. Prior to joining Stimson he had a distinguished career in the State Department and the Central Intelligence Agency (CIA), the last 10 years of which he spent at the National Intelligence Council (NIC). Burrows is one of the leading experts on strategic foresight and global trend analysis. He received a BA in American and European history from Wesleyan University and a PhD in European history from the University of Cambridge.

Dr. Josef Braml is the Secretary General of the German Group and the European Director of the Trilateral Commission—an influential global platform for dialogue between America, Europe and Asia. Previously from 2006 to 2020 he worked at the German Council on Foreign Relations (DGAP). He earned a PhD in Political Science and a Masters in International Business and Cultural Studies from the University of Passau.

To those seeking a new peaceful world

First published in the United Kingdom by Brixton Ink 2025
Copyright © Mathew Burrows and Josef Braml

Mathew Burrows and Josef Braml have asserted their rights under the Copyright Designs and Patents Act 1988 to be identified as the authors of this work

BRIXTON INK

Brixton Ink Limited Company Number 14823240
246 Stockwell Road, London, SW9 9SP, UK

Printed and bound in Great Britain by Clays Ltd Elcograf S.p.A.
A CIP catalogue record for this book is available from the British Library
ISBN 978-1-0685257-2-8

CONTENTS

Preface	7
Introduction: Terra Incognita	11

I.

Chapter 1: The End of the Dream	19

II.

Chapter 2: Russia and Europe under Trump	41
Chapter 3: From Chimerica to China Shock	58
Chapter 4: Rebalancing the Middle East	70
Chapter 5: Global South Left Out	78

III.

Chapter 6: War: No Longer Unthinkable	89
Chapter 7: Environmental Calamity: A Virtual Certainty	98
Chapter 8: Technology: The Best of Times?	104
Epilogue: Preparing for a New Age	115
Endnotes	125
Bibliography	143

PREFACE

Donald J. Trump's re-election surprised many who did not grasp his voter appeal and promise to change the status quo. Americans in a poll released shortly before the inaugural largely welcomed the return of Trump, giving his predecessor Joe Biden a record low approval.[1] Trump's landslide victory suggests that this is not just politics as usual but a result of a widespread disillusionment with existing institutions. Exploiting discontent in troubled times to gain power takes a certain sort of prodigy and a willingness to ignore conventional wisdom, customs and norms.

In hindsight, 20 January 2025, the day of Donald Trump's second inauguration, may be considered a historical turning point. Trump himself promised in his speech the beginning of a new, 'golden age of America'. 'From this day forward, our country will flourish,' he declared. 'During every single day of the Trump administration, I will, very simply, put America first.'[2]

The 45th and 47th president sees no limits to what he and his nation can achieve. Trump even wants Americans to pursue their 'manifest destiny into the stars', launching astronauts to plant the American flag on Mars. Yet he cares little for others on this planet. With Trump's second term, America has shifted away from the post-World War II liberal order that aimed to increase prosperity for both Americans and the global community.

As the former World Bank lead economist Branco Milanović observes,[3] these liberal principles were abandoned even before Trump's election. Neoliberal policies that were once popular have lost support, and this has contributed to political instability in Western countries, such as the United Kingdom, France and Germany—and, above all, the United States. Trump's assumption of power marks only a symbolic end to this era. He's the final blow to liberal economic principles and the rules-based world order which the US championed after the Second World War.

Regardless of personal opinions about Trump, his unconventional worldview will influence global dynamics. Simultaneously, the aspects of the emerging new world order that he and many others overlook will have implications for America and its foreign policy.

In the post-World War II era, globalisation, primarily driven by the US, has made the world more interconnected and interdependent. Today, some leading thinkers mistakenly underestimate the significance of this interconnectedness in politics, economics, culture and technology. It is also essential to consider the role of technological advancements and innovation in shaping our societies and the world to come. Additionally, we must recognise the rise of emerging powers and shifting alliances and discuss how these changes transform the geopolitical landscape and influence national and global governance. Understanding the dynamic nature of international power structures and how these shifts are creating a new world order is crucial.

The shift from a unipolar, US-dominated world order to a multipolar one marks a significant change in global politics. Multiple influential powers, including Russia, China and India, are rising. China's rapid economic growth and strategic partnership with Russia have increased its global influence. Organisations like BRICS (Brazil, Russia, India, China, and South Africa) highlight the cooperation among emerging powers challenging the Western-centric global governance system established after the Second World War, viewed as outdated by many Global South countries. These nations are pushing for reforms to reflect current economic and geopolitical realities. The relative decline of US dominance and the rise of other powers have created a more fragmented international order. This multipolar world presents both opportunities and risks. While it can lead to a more balanced distribution of power, it also requires careful navigation to avoid conflicts and ensure global stability.

This book prospects what lies ahead for America and the world. Under Trump's presidency, the future may not be entirely bleak. Achieving lasting peace in Ukraine and the Middle East and reducing tensions with China would greatly benefit the world. However, problems like climate change, which Trump dismisses, remain. Economists predict another financial downturn, potentially sparking significant changes. Rapid technological advances bring both risks and opportunities. Our book, written shortly before and after the US presidential elections in November 2024, addresses these issues, examining key countries and regions and broader global trends and impacts. While there are more detailed analyses available, this book offers a timely overview.

INTRODUCTION

Terra Incognita

'The old world is dying, and the new world struggles to be born: now is the time of monsters.'
Antonio Gramsci

With Donald Trump's second victory, America has closed the door on the post-World War II liberal order. It's been some time since US leaders and the American public believed in the effectiveness of the very multilateral institutions such as the United Nations, International Monetary Fund and World Bank that past US leaders created to ensure peace, stabilise the world economy and end global poverty.[1] That idealism persisted into the early years of the post-Cold War era when President Bill Clinton believed globalisation would lift all boats and that other nations would come to resemble America. With the end of the Cold War, democracy, free markets and American leadership were the destination for humanity in the US elite's 'end of history' dream world.

Washington was one of the first to be disabused, coming to see globalisation as a nightmare, accelerating the rise of its competitors. Whole industries and with them American jobs migrated to Mexico and China. The US sought to impose democracy in Iraq and Afghanistan, which went disastrously wrong. The 2008 financial crisis undermined US financial credibility and Americans' confidence in their own system: the financial sector—'too big to fail'—was bailed out while individuals were left struggling to hold on to homes and jobs.

The late 1990s saw the beginnings of a populist movement that Trump has masterfully exploited, leading him to the White House. Trump had all the hallmarks of his populist predecessors: he was straight-talking and made much of the fact that he was not a professional politician. His over-the-top language and in-your-face manner appealed to the disaffected and marginalised. His claims to wealth and business success captivated those who wanted a return of the American Dream.

His 2024 victory was even bigger than the 2016 one, attracting support from black and Hispanic men and the young besides the white working class. More working class voted for Trump than Kamala Harris, turning the Democrats into the party of the rich. Voters forgave him for the failures of his first term, particularly his mishandling of the pandemic. Few other politicians have understood the seismic economic and social changes that have made many give up on the American Dream. Inequality has grown to unprecedented heights.

Despite being born wealthy, he has been able to connect with the poor and disaffected. In the short term, he will make them feel good with lower taxes and an end to the influx of millions of so-called illegal immigrants who blue-collar workers feared would take away their jobs. Both parties have become enamoured with protectionism that could maroon US industry, ceding many industry sectors to China, particularly in green technologies. Trump is a pragmatist, so if his tariffs crater markets, he may try luring foreign businesses to America to take advantage of lower energy costs. That has a better chance of firing up manufacturing, but many of those new jobs will be taken by robots.

America must deal with its education system, which is failing to prepare workers for the Artificial Intelligence (AI) revolution. Over time, the AI revolution could be even worse for employment than the 'China Shock'—the effect of exploding Chinese exports on manufacturing employment in the West after China joined the World Trade Organisation in 2001—causing the loss of white-collar jobs as well as manual workers.

To train Americans for the coming changes in their working lives, the US government needs to invest extensively, despite the already tight budget situation. Neither party has a plan for curbing US fiscal deficits and debts, and both Republicans and Democrats are big spenders. The mounting debt is a time bomb. Trump is tempting fate with a slew of new tax reductions that could add trillions to the debt. He is betting that the inevitable reckoning does not happen on his watch.

Trump is under the illusion that higher customs revenues will compensate for the lack of revenue from tax breaks. He said at his inauguration that 'Instead of taxing our citizens to enrich other countries, we will tariff and tax foreign countries to enrich our citizens. For this purpose, we are establishing the External Revenue Service to collect all tariffs, duties, and revenues. It will be massive amounts of money pouring into our Treasury coming from foreign sources'.[2] For Trump, tariffs are an all-purpose weapon. Their threat alone is intended to persuade friends and foes alike to abide by US interests.

On foreign policy, Trump is a maverick and takes enjoyment from being outrageous, most recently musing about Canada becoming the 51st state—a total nonstarter—and using force to take over Greenland and the Panama Canal. People at home and abroad don't know whether to take him seriously but his tactics sometimes work to force an issue and get a negotiation underway, which will likely happen with the Danish government over a greater US presence in Greenland.[3] Despite his threats on Panama and Greenland, Trump has a fear of war that has disappeared among the US foreign policy elite.[4] Trump might succeed in stopping the fighting in Ukraine, but the Middle East has always been a hornet's nest, and he could ignite a broader regional conflict if he gangs up with Israel in attacking Iran. His belief that an economically strong America that he rebuilds will prevent other countries from waging war is naïve and delusional. Despite his aversion to war, Trump may not be able stop a march to war if tensions flare with China over Taiwan. As with Biden, the US primacy remains undisputed for Trump.

Under Trump, there might be less talk of war with China, but achieving harmony between the US and China seems improbable. Although Trump avoids hawkish neocons, he is still influenced by some anti-China advisers. His push to decouple from China will likely harm the US economy. Even if he doesn't fully proceed with 'decoupling', the chances for reviving global or regional trade are slim.

Trump's disregard for the plight of others will be overtime a problem for the West and an even bigger one in the near term for the Global South. Already Biden lost the plot about the developing world and Trump is even more ignorant. Africa and other developing countries are drowning in debt due to the pandemic's extra health costs. After globalisation lifted millions out of poverty, the numbers of poor are growing again while Western assistance declines.

There are now more interstate conflicts each year, most of which receive scant mention in the Western media. The ongoing

Myanmar civil war has seen over 50,000 dead and 3 million people displaced while the reignited Sudan internal conflict has resulted with almost 150,000 people killed in the past two years, along with over 3 million people displaced. Neither of these conflicts registered during the US election. Climate change and the associated struggle for increasingly scarce resources will exacerbate conflicts between and within states and the lack of Washington's concern will dent America's global leadership.

Trump believes climate change is a hoax, preferring to 'drill, baby, drill', as he repeated at his inaugural to secure fossil fuel independence. Nevertheless, on the current course, temperatures will likely rise to 2.9C above pre-industrial levels this century.[5] Like King Canute trying to hold back the tide, Trump's denialism won't keep the ever-more-powerful hurricanes from bashing the US Southeast or extinguish the wildfires across the western US, so vividly seen with the recent devastation of Los Angeles. Scientists already see a weakening of the Gulf Stream producing higher sea levels and the prospect—if it disappears—of freezing temperatures in North America and Europe. However, most of the climate burden will fall on poorer countries, which are more vulnerable to shocks and lack the resources to implement adaptation measures.

Trump pays little attention to the Global South. When the new president looks out on the world, he only sees the big players like China or Russia. The rest of the world is fuzzy to him and the idea that Global South countries are middle powers with a say in the global system is unfathomable. For him, you are either for or against the United States. Trump is unprepared for multipolarity.

It's unlikely that at the end of Trump's term, there will be any better reckoning with America's fading primacy in the international order. US diplomacy is not ready for concessions or compromises in building a new order based on the balance of power. Unipolarity—though out of date and no longer feasible—remains ingrained into the psyche of the foreign policy elite. Trump's desire to see less engagement in overseas wars may be positive but his disengagement from the world could tip over into a damaging isolationism.

The US needs global engagement to stay competitive, while the world relies on its power and ideas to tackle significant challenges. Domestically, the country will remain split after Trump leaves office even though he has brought more understanding of the plight of the working and middle classes. Even James Carville, the Democratic Party strategist who coined President Clinton's winning campaign slogan—'it's the economy, stupid'—has had to admit that 'Democrats ... flat-out lost the economic narrative' to Trump who 'decisively won by seizing a swath of middle-class and low-income voters focused on the economy'.[6] It will be up to a new post-Trump leader to unify America and, with it, make the changes needed for revising America's role in the world.

To return to the Gramsci quote that opens this chapter, at the end of his term, Trump won't be finished with taking apart the old order—the post-World War II order—nor will he be far down the path to rebuilding global cooperation. Like China's Xi and Russia's Putin, President Trump wants to break the old order. Much destruction will occur, but it's our profound hope and belief that a new, fairer world can come out of this chaos and that nations can build a new order that reboots global cooperation.

I.

CHAPTER 1

The End of the Dream

Many Americans don't feel they can get ahead, particularly among the lower middle and working classes and the young. For them, the system is rigged. The American Dream is now out of reach. The ones who took out loans to go to university because they were told that was the way to get ahead have found out that a non-science bachelor's degree has landed them with one after another low-paying job. With manufacturing declining, high school dropouts are stuck with minimum wage service jobs. The two major recessions—the 2007-08 financial crisis and the pandemic economic meltdown—catapulted many back to zero. Post-pandemic inflation made life unaffordable, even for many in the middle class. Increasingly Americans view themselves as losers.

Despite seeing themselves as classless, Americans are grappling with the reality of shrinking middle-class opportunities. For younger generations, surpassing their parents' or grandparents' success feels increasingly out of reach. The US middle class is shrinking.[1] This is often difficult to explain to outsiders, especially those whose standard of living is lower. They look on America as wealthy and successful. Indeed, the US median income is above most other countries.

It's hardwired into many Americans that if you work hard, you'll succeed. But there's a growing wealthy class that wants to perpetuate itself. The American elite fools itself into thinking that because the system is supposedly meritocratic, enjoying privileges is fine. But the system is far from meritocratic. Legacy students, sons or daughters of alumni get a leg up at Harvard and other top universities. A study by the National Bureau of Economic Research found that roughly 75 per cent of the white students admitted as legacies to Harvard would have been rejected without it.[2] The bad publicity surrounding this issue is causing some universities to renounce the idea, but so far Harvard and other elite colleges are sticking with it.

Where you grow up in America has been shown to determine your future income and life expectancy.[3] Growing up in poor or rural areas with badly run and under-resourced schools will cast a pall over your prospects. Americans hate to admit that upward mobility is beyond reach except for the rich and a lucky few, but the evidence is incontrovertible. The quantitative historian Peter Turchin writes that 'the relative wage of US workers increased robustly' in the 1960s, but from the 1970s onward, it declined and by 2010 had nearly halved. In 1983, there were only 66,000 households worth $10 million, but by 2019, their number had increased more than tenfold to 693,000. It shows the success of US capitalism, except for the fact that most Americans haven't seen their boat rise.

THE POPULIST TRADITION

Racism remains a significant lens through which many Americans, particularly liberals, understand social problems. While African Americans and other marginalised communities continue to face discrimination, recent research highlights disparities in socio-economic progress, with some minority groups making gains while many economically disadvantaged white Americans face worsening conditions.[4] Trump is wrong to downplay race, but he was right to shine a light on those falling out of the middle class. Besides broadening the base of the Republican Party with his message that the middle class is being trampled on, he reached out to minorities and the young more effectively than many of his predecessors.

There's a long populist tradition in America fuelled by a sense that a wealthy establishment is ignoring those on the lower rungs of society. In the late 19th century, populists, particularly those in the People's Party, opposed the gold standard, which they believed favoured the wealthy elite. They advocated for the use of silver to increase the money supply and make credit more accessible to farmers and working-class citizens. William Jennings Bryan's famous 'Cross of Gold' speech at the 1896 Democratic National Convention encapsulated this sentiment. Many populist movements also had exclusionary and nativist elements. The Know-Nothing Party, active in the mid-19th century, was a significant political force that opposed immigration, particularly from Catholic countries like Ireland. They feared that immigrants would undermine American values and take jobs from native-born citizens. Unlike historical populist movements, which often remained on the fringes or as third parties, Trump's modern populist movement has managed to take over a major political party. This shift has brought populist rhetoric and policies into the mainstream political discourse.

Trump's third presidential campaign was a re-run, emphasising the same anti-globalism and grievances of the working and middle classes. He won a bigger victory than in 2016, eating further into the Democratic Party's base by attracting blacks, Hispanics and the young. In 2016, there was shock. The earth moved under everyone's feet but when Biden won in 2020, Trump's first term was treated by the governing classes as an aberration that would never return. That is why there is again some disbelief. Yet Trump's actions in his first term may explain his victory and suggest how he will govern in his second term.

THE FIRST TERM

During his first term, Trump succeeded in lowering taxes by 9 to 56 per cent on the poorest to middle-income segments of American society.[5] He also reduced taxes on others in the upper middle class and rich between 8 to 12 per cent. The working and middle classes saw a rise in their standard of living before the pandemic, the memory of which fuelled Trump's popularity. Biden also deserves credit for bolstering middle- and lower-income households with the pandemic payouts to help the ailing economy. But the poor and middle class were squeezed the hardest by the post-pandemic inflation, with prices on many consumer essentials items going up 20 per cent since 2019. Wages rose too, but until 2023-24 they did not keep up with prices. With the poor and middle classes spending most of their income on food and rent, their memories of much lower prices were a source of anger.

With his tax reductions and increased expenditures, Trump

added to the debt during his first term. His corporate tax reductions did not lead to an investment boom, with many businesses complaining they were stymied by a lack of skilled workers. The Congressional Budget Office (CBO) forecasts federal debt will rise from 97 per cent of gross domestic product (GDP) at the end of fiscal year 2023 to a record 106 per cent of GDP by 2028 and to 166 per cent of GDP by 2054. Projected debt in 2054 will be more than double the pre-pandemic level as a share of the economy and 3.4 times the 50-year historical average of 48 per cent of GDP.[6]

Climate change will increase long-term fiscal risks. The CBO has highlighted that climate change could increase budget deficits over time. Investments in mitigation and adaptation are necessary to reduce these long-term costs.[7] Overall, climate change is projected to substantially impact the US economy, potentially leading to $2 trillion in lost revenue annually by the end of the century.[8]

The US government is expected to spend from $25 billion to $128 billion annually on disaster relief, flood insurance, crop insurance, healthcare, wildfire suppression and addressing flood risk at federal facilities. The increasing frequency and worsening intensity of extreme weather will drive these costs ever higher. For example, the budget for fiscal year 2024 included more than $23 billion for climate adaptation alone, in addition to investments in mitigation.[9]

These projections highlight the need to include climate risks in federal budgeting. However, Trump overlooks this. He and his close advisor and co-head of Department of Government Efficiency (DOGE), Elon Musk, envisage the opposite: huge cuts in domestic programmes, particularly those created under Biden such as subsidies for green tech. In his first term, Trump took the US out of the Paris Climate Accords, downgrading green energy and other technologies while promoting fossil fuels. The US went from a net energy importer to a liquefied natural gas exporter.[10] Natural gas is a less dirty fuel than oil or coal, but an energy policy focused on it risks delaying the green revolution.

Biden was a true believer in the future of renewables, but during his administration the US became the largest crude oil producer in the world, outstripping Russia, Saudi Arabia, and other members of the Organisation of Petroleum Exporting Countries (OPEC).[11] Despite Trump's charges that Biden has waged a war on US energy, his administration approved more permits for oil and gas drilling on public lands by October 2022 than his predecessor Trump had by the same point in his presidency.[12] However, in leaving office, Biden put in place a ban on all new oil and gas drilling along most of the US coasts[13] which Trump has promised to reverse.

Both Biden and Trump have tried to protect American markets and in doing so, increased inflation. In his first term, Trump slapped tariffs on steel and aluminum imports as well as on many manufactured goods from China. Biden eliminated some tariffs on products from Europe and Japan while keeping all the tariffs on China. In May 2024, as the presidential campaign was heating up, Biden hiked tariffs on an additional $18 billion of Chinese goods, including semiconductors and electric vehicles (EVs). The 100 per cent duty on EVs effectively eliminated their threat to US manufactured vehicles. But evidence shows US firms and consumers paid higher prices for the goods due to the Trump and Biden tariffs.[14] The cost of the tariffs for consumers has grown even higher under Biden.

A striking continuity between Trump and Biden showed the former's influence during his first term in turning America away from its traditional liberal path. Despite promising to wipe away everything his predecessor did, Biden took his cue from Trump on key issues. Biden did little to reform the World Trade Organisation, which became dysfunctional under Trump. Nor did Biden try to reboot world trade. Under Biden, as with Trump, the growth rate in trade slowed.[15]

Both Trump and Biden are believers in American exceptionalism but define it differently. For Biden, the US stands out due to its democratic values. The 'revolution of common sense' which Trump heralded in his inaugural speech[16] adds up to the separation of the US however and whenever its choses from the rest of the world. It's essentially a more brazen version of American exceptionalism that is already the prevalent belief of the political class. Trump no longer sugarcoats it. For him, winning, a word that peppered his address, is what matters.

Trump defines US power in economic terms. An economically powerful America that others cannot rival will keep the peace and avoid World War III, according to Trump's campaign statements.[17] He favours a strong military but as a deterrent. His idea of a military intervention is his in-and-out killing by a drone strike of Iran's Revolutionary Guard head, Qasem Soleimani, who was reportedly plotting attacks against US interests. Trump is a throwback to the Founders' notion of a US that abhorred 'foreign entanglements'.[18] While exceptional, the US is not for Trump an 'indispensable nation' righting every wrong in the world.[19] Trump sees that as economically wasteful, not helping ordinary Americans. He dislikes wars that endure—the 'forever wars' in Iraq and Afghanistan—and has criticised Israel's Prime Minister Benjamin Netanyahu for not wrapping up quickly the Gaza operations.

Some will welcome a US that steps aside, not waging unnecessary wars and bringing peace. Trump promised that America will no longer measure success by the battles it wins, 'but also by the wars that we end, and perhaps most importantly, the wars we never get into. My proudest legacy will be that of a peacemaker and a unifier, that's what I want to be, a peacemaker and a unifier'.[20]

It wouldn't be Trump, however, without contradictions. After promising to turn a leaf on American military adventurism, he vowed to get the Panama Canal back: 'We gave it to Panama, and we're taking it back'.[21] Elsewhere, he promised to do it, if necessary, by force. For Trump, the Monroe Doctrine, which claimed the whole Western hemisphere as a protected American domain, still prevails. Trump praised President William McKinley as a forgotten great president who waged a war against Spain and won Cuba and The Philippines.

AFTER TRUMP

Despite the media view that Trump's election changes everything, mostly for the worse, a new administration could bring about some positive shifts, while also kicking many of the country's thorniest problems onto the next presidency.

Trump inherits a strong economy with lower inflation. The renewal of his tax cuts plus additional measures to help workers, such as no tax on tips, are likely to pass given Republican control over Congress. Ending taxes on social security payments, which would bolster Trump's standing with seniors, will probably have to be pared back because of worries about the system's long-term viability.

Trump's help for the working class is overdue. Still, he won't solve America's gross inequality problem without reforming inheritance laws, something he opposes, and better equipping the children of the working class to compete in a knowledge economy. Biden and Trump have all but ignored the problem of education. Losses in basic English and mathematics from when students were out of school during the pandemic have yet to be made up in the years since.[22] The US has the best universities in the world, but the quality of primary and secondary schools varies enormously. America was successful in the 20th century partly because workers were much better educated than their foreign counterparts. After the Second World War, the postwar GI bill helped veterans go to university but, in recent decades, the education level of workers in competing countries has improved and America no longer has an advantage.

Making things worse for the US labour market and creating an additional inflationary pressure, Trump promises to deport 11 to 12 million undocumented migrants. In a break with tradition and the US Constitution, Trump will reportedly try to end birthright citizenship for US-born children whose parents lack legal immigration status.[23] The final number forced to leave is likely to be a fraction of this aim, possibly one to two million. Finding them will be the first problem as they are spread across the country, shielded by many high-growth 'sanctuary cities' and businesses eager for inexpensive labour.

Trump's deportation policies may significantly impact industries that rely on immigrant labour.[24] The agricultural sector, where 50 to 70 per cent of farmworkers are undocumented, could face severe labour shortages, resulting in unharvested crops and higher food prices. The construction industry could see delays and increased costs due to exacerbated labour shortages. The hospitality sector, including hotels and restaurants, might experience higher operating costs, reduced services, or closures. Deportations could also disrupt the meatpacking and food processing supply chain, decreasing the availability of meat and dairy products. Overall, these policies could increase business costs, consumer prices and cause economic disruptions.

According to a chief executive of two technology companies, a 'mass deportation would create an immediate crisis in the tech sector, where immigrant talent drives innovation'.[25] Late in 2024, a split opened up among Republicans over H1B visas that allow American employers to hire foreign workers in key specialty occupations. Elon Musk strongly favours the retention and expansion of the H1B visa programme, arguing on his social media platform X that 'the number of people who are super talented engineers AND super motivated in the USA is far too low'.[26] Siding with Musk but alienating many of his supporters, Trump has also admitted he has used workers with H1B visas in his businesses. Despite pressure from tech and other industries for an expansion of the H1B visa programme, Congress has failed to raise the 85,000 cap.

Deporting undocumented migrants will damage ties with Latin America compounding already tense relations. Trump wants to physically cutoff the US from its southern neighbours, using the military to seal the southern border. 'All illegal entry will immediately be halted,' he said in his inaugural speech, 'and we will begin the process of returning millions and millions of criminal aliens back to the places from which they came.'[27]

Trump claims to have the prerogative to tell others what to call the Gulf of Mexico which he has decided to unilaterally re-baptise as the 'Gulf of America'. In his inaugural speech, Trump also declared a national emergency at the US-Mexican border. He emphasised using the US military to address what he described as 'forms of invasion', including illegal migration and drug trafficking.[28] Trump's team has reportedly been debating a counter-invasion into Mexico, an effort to clear out the drug lords on Mexico's side of the border; the very threat from the new US president would be inflammatory and risk bilateral ties.[29] Trump has already threatened tariffs against Mexico. The US needs

Mexico to stop the caravans of migrants from Central America who travel through Mexico to America's southern border.

Deportations could create an even greater division within the country, which Trump, like other incoming presidents, has pledged to unify. A majority of Americans have mixed opinions; they generally believe immigrants contribute positively to society and oppose deporting all undocumented immigrants, with the exception of those who have committed crimes.[30]

Just days after the elections, several state governors vowed to fight deportations. Unless Trump attracts bipartisan Congressional support, there is no guarantee of an immigration reform bill that would prioritise the skilled migrants that Trump favours over those with family ties. Prior legislation has always drawn support from both sides of the aisle, requiring concessions. Trump ignores the fact that the US population will begin to decline in the 2030s without immigration. Businesses, including technology firms, have thrived because of a young, immigrant workforce.

Despite the shortage of skilled labour that have plagued tech industries, even highly sought and subsidised ones like the Taiwan Semiconductor Manufacturing Company's Arizona microchip plant,[31] Biden and Trump have been dreaming about a manufacturing boom. Biden passed unprecedented subsidies, attracting huge investments from European and Asian companies, but at the end of his administration, no new manufacturing jobs were added except for the ones that bounced back from the pandemic. Trump has promised to lure foreign companies to relocate in America without subsidies.

While some may come, the US and the West will lose time in the battle against China, which will be producing the next generation of EVs, solar panels, wind turbines and batteries. Even those firms attracted by low energy costs will set up highly automated factories, employing a fraction of the workers of older industries.

American green tech companies will be protected against Chinese firms with tariffs but won't probably be competitive globally. The subsidies that Biden introduced will be cut back under Trump. For Republicans, climate change ranked last among the 20 priority areas that they thought the next president must concern himself with.[32] Trump has appointed Chris Wright, the chief executive of a fracking company and critic of climate change efforts, as his Department of Energy secretary. He clearly has no interest in renewables and wants the US to be a fossil fuel superpower. Trump withdrew the US, again, from the Paris Agreement and slowed the transition to a zero-carbon economy by loosening requirements on US companies, including automakers. 'We will be a rich nation again,' Trump promised in his inaugural speech, 'and it is that liquid gold under our feet that will help to do it. With my actions today, we will end the Green New Deal, and we will revoke the Electric Vehicle Mandate, saving our auto industry.'[33]

The timing of Trump's election could not have been worse for bolstering US and Western leadership on climate. There has been a crescendo of criticism from developing countries about the lack of help. It will only grow louder. On this, China will be seen as the indispensable nation, not the US. After four more years of US inactivity, even a Democratic successor will struggle to catch up with China. Trump doesn't care, but future generations of Americans are likely to feel the loss of leadership on this issue as there will be more extreme and costlier weather events such as the Los Angeles fires, meaning greater burdens on federal and state governments, insurers and households.

Trump's campaign pledge to put 10 to 20 per cent tariffs on all imports plus an additional 50 per cent on Chinese goods will also send inflation higher, hurting workers and the middle class. He may have to pare back and settle for more 'managed trade' deals with China and Europe, forcing them to buy more American products. The 'Buy America' protectionism policies, which limit the federal government's ability to purchase cheaper imported goods, will also have a significant impact on inflation.[34] A study from the Peterson Institute for International Economics calculated that a feasible package of trade liberalisation measures, including a relaxation of 'Buy America' rules, 'could deliver a one-time reduction in consumer price index inflation of around 1.3 percentage points'.[35]

ENDING WARS

Trying to reduce US expenditures, Trump is intent on ending the Ukraine war, having been vocal in blaming Biden for letting it start. He may have an added reason for trying to find a solution. Trump wants to reduce European dependence on the US for its security. Ending the fighting in Ukraine is the first step. Moreover, there is growing Republican opposition to assistance for Ukraine, which could help get both sides to the table. Russian forces continue to advance, slowly taking more territory and reducing the opposition in Kyiv to working with Trump on a ceasefire agreement. Soon after the election, Russian President Vladimir Putin said he was open to hearing more about Trump's plans but if his forces continue to advance, particularly if part of the Ukrainian defences collapse, Putin will want to grab more land in the south and east before agreeing to a ceasefire.

Ceasefires, let alone broader peace agreements, are notoriously hard to negotiate, and this war has more complications than most. Trump will face domestic and allied opposition if he concedes too much to Russia, such as denying Ukraine membership in NATO and forcing it to be neutral. Even if Trump denies Zelensky's wish for NATO membership, Putin will likely want assurances against substantial NATO assistance in arms, intelligence and training. The New START treaty expires in 2026, and Trump has intimated an interest in reviving arms control. While lessening the security commitment to Europe is popular with many Republicans, getting Congressional backing for talks on a new arms control agreement with Russia would require a permanent ceasefire and at least the prospect of a fuller settlement.

A ceasefire agreement with peacekeepers and a demilitarised zone looks possible by the end of Trump's second term. However, given the hurdles, a way forward to a more permanent peace in Europe and arms control with Russia and China appears unlikely. Other conflicts, like Korea, have never been settled with a full peace accord, just an armistice, and yet have remained mostly calm.

THE MIDDLE EAST

The situation in the Middle East is even more volatile. It has changed dramatically since Trump's first term when there was relative peace, and he succeeded in getting several Arab states to recognise Israel in return for trade relations. Trump has been anti-Iran and agrees with Israel on the need to stop any renewed Iranian push on nuclear weapons. However, the risk is that his presidency could be overwhelmed, and his economic programme would be derailed by too heavy an involvement in the Middle East.

Biden's backing for Israel in its Gaza campaign divided America. The demonstrations over Israeli actions show the extent to which Americans' support for Israel, even among younger Jews, is fraying. In public surveys, American support for Palestinians still ranks below support for Israel but younger generations are less sympathetic to Israel. What they see is Palestinian suffering. International opinion is now on the side of the Palestinians and Biden's support brought charges of hypocrisy because of US criticism of Russia's similar actions in Ukraine.

Republicans are traditionally enthusiastic supporters of Israel. Trump has appointed former Arkansas Governor Mike Huckabee, an evangelical Christian who is sympathetic to the idea of Israel annexing the West Bank and Gaza. Trump also appointed real estate mogul Steve Witkoff as his Middle East envoy.[36] Even the Biden White House acknowledged Witkoff's contribution to helping the mid-January diplomatic talks which resulted in a ceasefire agreement between Hamas and the Israeli government.[37]

Just as Biden lost credibility and popularity with his Israel policy and his bungled exit from Afghanistan, Trump could set off a firestorm at home and throughout the international community if he gives the green light for an Israeli government to annex Palestinian territories. Most of the world, and many Americans, would see this as a flagrant violation of international law. Moreover, Trump would sacrifice his plans for Saudi normalisation of ties with Israel. Despite sweeteners like a defence pact with the US, Riyadh would lose its standing in the Muslim world if it made such a Faustian bargain.

Moreover, supporting Israel won't remove the Iranian threat. There's worry already that Tehran may make a dash for nuclear weapons. Such a pro-Israel strategy by Trump could reinforce those in Iran who want to take the final step toward nuclear weapons. Trump might be better off opening talks with Tehran—as he has suggested at times in the campaign.[38] This would require tempering some of the enthusiasm among

Republicans for bashing Iran and heightening Israeli hegemony in the Middle East.

Blocking Iran's oil exports to China, which Trump claims fund Iran's allies like Hezbollah, Hamas and the Houthis, would be risky. Beijing and Tehran have developed a trading system that uses the Chinese currency, the yuan, and involves a network of middlemen, making sanctions enforcement difficult. Russia, Iran's increasingly close partner, could re-pay the arms assistance Tehran has provided for its fight in Ukraine by supplying even more (advanced) missile technology. Moscow and Tehran have a mutual interest in evading Western sanctions imposed on both countries. A few days before Trumps second inauguration, Putin and his Iranian counterpart, Masoud Pezeshkian, signed a 20-year strategic-partnership treaty in Moscow. The pact will deepen economic, energy and defence co-operation. Finally, Iranian threats to close the Straits of Hormuz would send oil prices higher just when Trump's tariffs may already be causing inflation. America no longer has uncontested power in the Middle East. Russia and China are increasingly players, and Trump's efforts to take on Iran would only further empower the Russia-North Korea-Iran-China axis.

As the Chinese often say in their discussions with Americans, the Middle East is a graveyard of empires. In the first decades of the 21st century, the US damaged its standing as a global leader by getting into hopeless wars trying to remake the Middle East and Central Asia. Presidents from Jimmy Carter onwards who have waded too far into the Middle East morass got burnt, and their other policy aspirations at home and abroad were often obliterated. Trump risks going down the same path.

REST OF THE WORLD

While the United States was engaged in wars in Iraq and Afghanistan, China was cultivating what would come to be called the Belt and Road Initiative (BRI). This scheme represents one of the most ambitious foreign policy and investment plans ever conceived. It aims to create direct land and sea links between China's industrial heartlands and Europe, the Middle East and Africa.

China, along with Russia, was fiercely opposed to the Iraq War, yet it became one of its primary beneficiaries. In 2008, the China National Petroleum Corporation signed a production deal with the Iraqi government, becoming the first foreign firm to do so since the war. By 2013, China had bought almost half of Iraqi oil production.[39] This strategy allowed China to secure vital energy resources and expand its regional influence. Moreover, Iraq has become a key partner in BRI. In 2021, Iraq received $10.5 billion, making it the third-biggest BRI energy partner, after Russia and Pakistan.[40] This investment includes projects such as the Al-Khairat heavy oil power plant near Karbala and the development of the Mansuriya gas field. BRI has significantly increased China's influence in the Global South, particularly in regions where the US dropped its focus.

Trump and other Republicans still talk of the 'Third World', and an understanding of the Global South's, or the Global Majority's, growing power has not penetrated their thinking. Ironically, Trump and Global South leaders share a similar view of national sovereignty but for different reasons. Trump wants the US to be the wealthiest, most economically powerful nation, one that is largely self-sufficient but can throw its weight around, forcing other countries to do what it wishes. Global South leaders are also intent on building up their countries so that they will never be subjected to colonialism again. It's not just China that endured a 'century of humiliation' by Western colonisers.

Neither China nor Europe can supplant the US, which means that the fragmentation of the global economy will continue and likely intensify under Trump. This trend is expected to reduce economic growth, with the developing world being the most adversely affected. The poorest countries will also bear the brunt of worsening climate devastation, unless they get increased assistance. Without it, climate change will accelerate problems, increasing the number of conflicts and fuelling migration. The lack of an open global economy into which developing countries can sell their products could see more failed states that have been breeding grounds for insecurity. Although terrorism and insurgencies are still destructive elements that threaten peace, recent editions of the US National Security Strategy have downgraded the threat of non-conventional wars. Not long ago, after the terrorist attacks of 11 September 2001, Western governments were more concerned with failing states than with interstate conflicts.

ROLLING BACK CHINA

Trump's views on China differ from most others in the US foreign policy elite. It's not that he is for and they're against, but his grievances are mainly economic—America's trade deficits and loss of manufacturing jobs. Biden and many others saw it as an ideological contest over democracy versus authoritarianism. Whether Trump can permanently change the tone and trajectory away from the growing tensions is unclear. Washington's elites have formed a consensus around opposition to China, an attitude driven by economic and political concerns.

Increasingly for the Washington foreign policy elite, it is about whether Taiwan stays in the US orbit or not. During the recent presidential campaign, Trump dodged the question of whether he would defend Taiwan, saying that 'Taiwan should pay us for defence'. As he put it, 'You know, we're no different than an insurance company.'[41] It may be a relief for Beijing to haggle over trade, not a fundamental issue like Taiwan.

Beijing appears confident that it can manage a second Trump presidency. Secretary of State Marco Rubio is a China hawk. Still, unlike Mike Pompeo, who held the office in the previous Trump administration, Rubio is a realist and an admirer of China's accomplishments who is not after regime change. He wants the United States to compete better with China. A deal to lower the US trade deficit, as happened at the end of Trump's last term, is a possible way out of tariffs that would risk inflation. China would have to buy more from the US but would not face an implacably hostile administration opposed to CCP rule.

Nevertheless, Chinese leaders resent Washington's hostile rhetoric and above all fear Trump's unpredictability. In that vein, worried that Trump could be laying a trap, Xi did not accept the new president's invitation to attend the January inaugural.[42] Xi doesn't want a war any more than Trump and is consumed with trying to navigate a difficult economy. Besides the threat of higher tariffs or complete decoupling, Trump could raise tensions with Beijing by engaging other governments in a coordinated effort to stop the flood of Chinese exports.

Because China has risen as an economic and military rival to the US, and Washington is increasingly orienting itself towards Asia, Europe should be prepared for a de-globalised world economy and work towards being able to defend itself. With Trump's return to the White House, Europeans will have to spend more on defences against a revanchist Russia and on the reconstruction of Ukraine. Under commander-in-chief Trump, NATO and the US promise of protection to Europe can no longer be taken for granted.

ALLIANCES MATTER LESS

The message from Trump will be that allies must be more self-reliant for their security. Trump has said that he won't pull the US out of NATO, but US forces could be withdrawn from the region, particularly if the Middle East crisis worsens. If so, he will expect European allies to defend themselves against Russia, which could cause increased tensions.

Just as America is split, European domestic audiences and governments won't be happy going along with Trump unless US Middle East policy becomes more even-handed. Europeans are more sympathetic to the Palestinians than most Americans, and Trump's full backing of Israel could raise transatlantic tensions.

Despite plans to put tariffs on European exports to the United States, the Trump administration will try to argue that curbing Chinese exports should be a common cause. Western governments should draw lessons from the Cold War and strive to prevent a recurrence of such tensions. However, obstacles to de-globalisation are diminishing. The world is entering a new confrontational era, with Western rivalry against China and Russia driven by increasing barriers and protectionism.

II.

CHAPTER 2

Russia and Europe Under Trump

The West constantly misjudges Russia. The CIA did not see the collapse of the Soviet Union coming. The United States and Western governments had better intelligence before the Ukraine war, but for too many, it was still a shock that Russia would invade. Historical parallels, such as Napoleon's invasion of Russia, highlight the challenges of predicting Russian responses. The French emperor won the pivotal battle at Borodino and expected the Russians to accede to French terms, becoming a client state. We know the ending to those plans, along with Hitler's. Despite the revolution and a debilitating civil war, Stalin sat comfortably, smug and smiling at the 1945 Yalta Summit while a sick Roosevelt and a downcast Churchill sat at his sides.

Russia is not a nation that makes much sense to the West. Its geopolitical strategy often defies Western expectations, rooted in a distinct historical and cultural context. There have been four empires,[1] rising and falling, each one morphing into another. Britain may have had two empires, but both were colonial and commercially based. Russia's have been territorial, spanning two continents. For a while, in the 18th century and early 19th century, when it was an ally against Napoleon, it was seen as Western, sharing in the Enlightenment. Then, after the Congress of Vienna, which marked the high point of Russian prestige, it did not march toward democracy like Europe and America. The West has oscillated between condemnation and belittlement, from time to time seeking Russia's help. France needed it to balance a rising Germany before World War I. The Allies wanted its help in both world wars.

Since the Cold War's end, the West has largely belittled Russia. George W. Bush may have looked into Putin's eyes and seen his soul, but his administration pushed for Ukraine and Georgia to be admitted to NATO. Barack Obama irked Putin by calling Russia a shrinking 'regional power'. There was widespread shock when Putin annexed Crimea. The second invasion of Ukraine was less surprising. After an initially unsuccessful assault, Russia now holds the upper hand in a war of attrition.

Putin is fighting a war we don't understand. In our eyes, it's a throwback to the wars fought for or against German and Italian national unification in the 19th century. Putin hires ethnic mercenaries, who are paid what seems to them to be a fortune. Their families benefit when they sign up and again if they are killed. Despite Western sanctions, the Russian economy keeps ticking along, if not thriving. Putin quickly assembled a black fleet of aged tankers to transport his oil and found new markets for gas. It's not just China but India—which the West has encouraged to become an ally—that is a big buyer of Russian oil.

The West needs to shed its preconceptions about Russia; it is adapting faster than the West to the changing multipolar world. The West is right to think that Russia is a pale version of the Soviet Union. For all of Putin's nostalgia, he knows Russia will never regain that status. Unlike the West, which has comforted itself for most of the past 30 years that history has stopped, Russian thinkers—in part because of the economic hardships that accompanied the Soviet collapse—started early on theorising about an end to US hegemony, constructing a different concept for the world around the idea of multipolarity, or polycentrism, as they call it.

There were good strategic reasons for Russia to invade Ukraine. Its Black Sea Fleet is anchored at Sevastopol on the Crimean Peninsula. With the exit of the pro-Russian leader Viktor Yanukovych at the time of the 2014 Maidan uprising in Kyiv, it was only a matter of time, as Putin saw it, before the new Ukrainian government demanded the departure of his fleet, closing off Moscow's outlet to the Mediterranean. Putin, who compares himself to Russia's past tsars, knew that acquiring that port had been the ambition of a long string of tsars before Catherine II achieved it in the 18th century. If he did not seize Crimea, he would go down as the leader who lost access to the Middle East and Africa.

PUTIN'S ASPIRATIONS

So long as Russia is winning in Donbas, in eastern Ukraine, Putin may not want to settle, but he probably knows the war cannot go on forever without jeopardising his country's future. Increasingly polls indicate that Russians want peace, but one that is not a humiliating surrender.[2] Once Donbas has been taken and other parts of southern Ukraine are fully under Russian control, the public may get more anxious. Another call-up—even if most of the recruits come from outside Moscow and St Petersburg—

would increase public disquiet. The longer growth is fuelled by defence spending, the harder it will be to switch back to a peace economy. China, India and other countries that have thrown a lifeline to Russia don't like the war and want it to end as soon as possible. Once most of Donbas is secured, Putin will likely come under increasing pressure from all sides.

Despite what Putin has said publicly about preferring the Democrats, Trump will be more obliging to Putin than any other Western leader. Trump doesn't have any grudges against Russia and admires Putin as a tough leader. Russia poses no economic threat to the US, which is what concerns Trump most. He does not feel beholden to NATO and is sympathetic to Putin's opposition to Ukraine's membership in the alliance.

Any NATO member can veto applicants, and Trump would not face a major backlash if he did this to Ukraine. After all, Biden also held back from such a commitment, despite pressure from European allies. Biden, like Trump, knew the American public would not stand being sucked into a major war with Russia. NATO membership would mean that the US would have to prepare for such an eventuality, and Europeans would not have to worry about being left on their own defending Ukraine.

Sanctions are a different story. During Trump's first term, Democrats in Congress, along with many in Trump's party, ganged up on the president and passed sanctions legislation against Russia that would require congressional approval to lift. Trump would not be able to relax them unless Congress agreed.

Despite his current rhetoric, Putin doesn't believe the US will soon lift all its sanctions and therefore the Russian leader is unlikely to make their total removal a pre-condition for negotiations.[3] Putin will instead want a commitment that Ukraine will not join NATO. Putting a 20-year limit on the promise to keep Ukraine out will probably not work with Putin who remembers the pledges that Boris Yeltsin received from George H.W. Bush that NATO would not be extended towards Russia's borders. Putin will reiterate demands to reduce NATO troops and pre-positioning of equipment on his frontiers.

Restarting arms control talks would have advantages for both sides, reducing the risks of a collision and the costs of a continuous build-up. Putin may be worried about seeing the New START agreement expire in 2026. He has suspended it, not renounced it. Biden sought new arms control talks, but Putin refused amid his ongoing war effort. A new arms race would be costly for Russia when the defence budget has ballooned, and health and education budgets have been cut. Putin is now talking about replacing Russia's flat tax on income with higher taxes on the wealthy. Increased expenditures on new nuclear weapons would see Russia's economy follow that of the Soviet Union, with a vast share permanently devoted to defence.

For Trump, there are also domestic concerns which could lead him to negotiate. The costs of the current modernisation of US nuclear forces are way over their original estimates and are likely to exceed $1 trillion. Trump has favoured boosting defence spending, but he has also promised an array of costly domestic initiatives, as well as tax cuts. With an aging population, health care costs are growing, as is pension spending. For Trump, an arms race against Russia and China is unlikely to be welcome if it means backing off on some of his campaign promises.

Russia and the United States have similar stockpiles of nuclear weapons. China, however, has been building up its nuclear weaponry, and while still below US and Russian levels, it is becoming a much more important nuclear actor. While circumspect, Russian experts have said China should be part of arms control talks, but Putin probably wants to be the chief interlocutor with the US on this issue.

UKRAINE'S SECURITY

Ukraine will need security guarantees too if there is to be peace.[4] In the May 2022 draft agreement between Russia and Ukraine that was never consummated, there was a plan for all five Security Council members—the US, China, France, Russia and the UK—and other guarantor states to be obliged, following consultations with Ukraine and among themselves, to help the nation. Russia would not have a veto on this. Remarkably, these obligations were spelled out with much greater precision than NATO's Article 5 under which an attack on one is an attack on all. It allowed for 'imposing a no-fly zone, supplying weapons, or directly intervening with the guarantor state's own military force'.[5]

Russia has not been opposed to Ukraine becoming a member of the European Union, and in the 2022 draft agreement, Russia even promised to discuss the status of Crimea with Kyiv in 10 to 15 years. In May 2022, the initial Russian invasion had failed. It's very doubtful Putin or even a successor would agree now to any discussion of Crimea, but Russia's willingness then may suggest that some negotiation over Russian-held territory in other parts of Ukraine is not out of the question.

Should Russia break a negotiated ceasefire, NATO allies would need to be clear and open about their commitment to Ukraine's defence. Academic research has shown that there are few cases of peace failing when an outside state has explicitly underwritten the ceasefire. Peacekeepers also lengthen the duration of any ceasefire.[6] Peacekeepers would need to be recruited from neutral, third-party countries, as Putin isn't likely to allow any European troops to be monitors of the peace. Creating a demilitarised zone at least two kilometres wide running the length of the ceasefire line would also decrease the risk of renewed conflict.

Beyond a durable peace, Ukraine would need help from Bretton Woods institutions—the World Bank and the IMF—and bilateral assistance for reconstruction. For this, the ceasefire agreement would have to guarantee Ukraine's and others' access to shipping lanes in the Black Sea. For its part, Beijing has offered to provide substantial help once peace occurs. Not including China in a global reconstruction coalition would risk Beijing's undermining conditionality with Belt and Road Initiative-type investment.

PUTIN'S PIVOT

Western sanctions now serve Putin's purpose of re-orienting Russians to the East. In Peter the Great's reign, he moved the capital to a windswept swamp off the Baltic Coast as part of his efforts to be more European. Putin wouldn't move the capital, but Russia, having had its economic ties cut with Europe, relies now on China, India and others in the Global South as markets for energy and mineral exports. Putin is making this switch permanent; Russia is expanding transportation infrastructure, including pipelines connecting it with China, Iran and the Global South.

Russia's pivot to the East was announced during his 2012 presidential campaign, pre-dating the Ukraine war, and the West initially dismissed it. Two-way Sino-Russian trade has now exploded. In 2023, China bought half of Russia's oil and petroleum products.[7] Chinese cars have replaced European models across Russia. Moscow has rapidly increased the yuan's share in its reserves and switched to direct ruble-yuan trade.

Since 2014, Russia has laid more than 2,000 kilometres of railway tracks and renovated more than 5,000 kilometres of the Trans-Siberian Railway and the Baikal-Amur Mainline. Another 3,100 kilometres of track is planned for the next eight years, which will help Moscow meet international demand for resources from its east.

China and Russia are building additional transport links to facilitate their growing trade. In 2022, a vehicle bridge over the Amur River, the Russo-Chinese boundary line, was opened along with the only railway bridge connecting the two countries. These shorten the journey between Moscow and China's Heilongjiang region by over 800 kilometres, saving 10 hours of transit time. A second railway bridge over the Amur is planned, providing the resource-rich Sakha Republic with direct access to China, eliminating the need for sea transport.

India is exploring more cooperation on Far East and Arctic transit links, but New Delhi is less invested with Moscow than Beijing. Moscow and New Delhi have started work on the Vladivostok-Chennai Eastern Maritime Corridor, which will include connections with Vietnam, Thailand and Indonesia while linking to the Northern Sea Route. Prime Minister Narendra Modi and Putin signed a cooperation programme for the Russian Far East for 2024-29. Nevertheless, India has shied away from long-term energy contracts despite buying more of Russia's discounted oil than China in recent times.

Another project is a North–South Corridor, a planned railway route that will connect Russia to the Indian Ocean via Iran that has been in the making since 2005 and will likely drag on for some time. Desirous of a southern outlet other than through the Bosphorus, Russia continues to loan funding to the Iranians to complete the remaining gap.

Russia's big ambition is the development of the Northern Sea route via the Arctic Sea, which would cut the time to ship Chinese goods to Europe through the Suez Canal by almost half.

Much of Russia's original plans for extracting its Arctic resources involved the West. European shipping companies mostly cut ties with Russian operators in 2022, and Western energy companies abandoned their energy projects.

Both Putin and Xi have a fascination with the new Arctic route. Putin sees in the Arctic a new narrative about conquering nature. The Arctic is a pathway to Russia's return to great power status. For Xi, the Northern Sea route is the one maritime artery that isn't controlled by the US fleet; others such as the Malacca and Taiwan straits are vulnerable to a US blockade.

Perhaps Russia's biggest challenge remains attracting people to such a forbidding environment. Compared to other northern regions—Alaska, Greenland, Scandinavia—Russia's Arctic population has decreased. There was a 20 per cent decline at the end of the Soviet period and a continuing net outflow of about 18,000 residents per annum. The population, currently approximately 2.4 million, is growing in some areas while declining in others.[8]

The opening of the Northern Sea Route will solidify Russo-Chinese ties. Russia and China have signed an agreement to design and construct new ice-class container ships. More than any far-off global shipping potential, the Northern Sea route will be used to exploit and transport energy and minerals, of which there is an abundance. The region has an estimated 13 per cent of the world's undiscovered oil and 30 per cent of undiscovered natural gas.[9]

Russia's breaking away from the West does face some challenges. Russian elites worry about the growing dependence on Beijing. Beneath the veneer of friendliness, many Russians are distrustful of the Chinese and its economic reliance on Western markets. In Russian eyes, China hasn't broken ties with the West, as Russia has been forced to do. For the next decade, if not longer, Russians have few options but their growing reliance on China even if they have started to boost activity in other parts of Asia, the Middle East, and Africa. With an increasing network of rail, energy pipelines and sea routes, they are laying the foundations for new Russian links in the East and South.

Putin could remain in power under Russia's constitution until 2036. In his early 70s, Putin's health has been a subject of rumours for years. The CIA has reportedly produced classified assessments that Putin is suffering from advanced cancer. Its director, Bill Burns, appeared to dismiss such concerns at a 2022 conference where he said that Putin was 'entirely too healthy'.[10] Even if he does have some sort of cancer, other leaders such as French president Francois Mitterrand have outlived their doctors' prognoses. It was only weeks after his election in 1981 that Mitterrand was diagnosed with aggressive prostate cancer and told he had only months to live. He served 14 years in office.

Even if he has a serious illness, Putin will try his best to hang on until the Ukraine crisis is resolved in Russia's favour. He probably distrusts any future leader to be as determined as he has been to keep Ukraine out of NATO and fully integrate Russian-speaking regions such as Donbas into Russia. It's unlikely another leader would have taken the gamble of war, and Putin would not want to retire to his dacha to see his legacy frittered away, as happened to Mikhail Gorbachev, who lived to see Russia turn its back on democracy.

Putin may not have a choice. Fate often intervenes, as so many Russian novels tell us. Most successors to authoritarians are authoritarians. Another Gorbachev would be too much to count on. Still, Putin's successor will probably want to re-balance Russia back towards the West, mainly to gain access to Western financial markets and reopen economic ties. Reliance on fossil fuel exports for government revenue and stoking the economy for defence purposes is not a good long-term bet.

China is funding much of the Russian energy infrastructure, but a successor will want to lessen dependence on China and diversify investment streams. The Russian economic future is bleak on present fundamentals, with a declining population and little funding for scientific research beyond military purposes. Russia has options both in the West and East but, as one of Putin's cabinet ministers said to a coauthor, it has been harder for Russia to deal diplomatically with the West than the East over the past few centuries. A new leader without the keen memories of the awful 1990s might be less reluctant to reengage, but Russia will likely always remain ambivalent about the West.

Inserting a wedge between Russia and China has a precedent in the Cold War when the Soviet Union and China came to blows, and Beijing was worried about a Soviet nuclear attack. President Nixon seized the opportunity to forge an opening to China. It is unlikely that Russia and China can be pulled apart today with the US having better ties with each than they do with each other. Yet walling off Russia will only push it closer to China.

EUROPE'S THREATS

Certainly, Europe will never go back to relying so heavily on cheap natural gas from Russia even if import restrictions are eased after the war's end. Putin's second invasion of Ukraine in February 2022 shattered Europe's belief in Moscow as a reliable partner. In the absence of sufficient renewable energies such as solar and wind power, Europe keeps trying to find alternative energy sources, including the use of liquefied natural gas (LNG) from the Middle East and the US.

In 2023, the United States became the world's largest LNG

exporter, surpassing Qatar after just eight years in the export business.[11] Yet on 26 January 2024, the Biden administration announced a pause on new permits for LNG exports to non-free trade agreement countries,[12] unsettling European allies. Energy Secretary Jennifer Granholm stated that the US Department of Energy needed to update economic, environmental and national security analyses.[13] In an election year, Biden aimed to please the domestic environmental community while gaining leverage with European allies needing 'freedom gas' after losing Russian supplies. Trump, however, is counting on Europeans to buy American LNG even as he threatens to reduce US military support for Europe.

Trump's comeback poses significant economic risks to Europe. Dealmaker Trump cares less than Biden about environmental aspects but he knows how to use energy supplies and assurances of protection to force Europeans to make economic concessions. The second Trump administration could strain transatlantic relations by cutting US military aid to Ukraine, reducing support for NATO, and imposing tariffs, potentially sparking a trade war. Even if Trump does not directly target its economy, Europe will find itself in the crossfire of the Sino-US rivalry, which might also undermine its unity.

EUROPE'S ABSENCE

The Ukraine war initially united Europe and improved ties with the United States. However, political and economic divisions in Europe are emerging, along with weakening leadership and reduced competitiveness. Europe is struggling to support Ukraine as Russia gains military advantage. While North Korea has dispatched an estimated 11,000 soldiers to help Putin's war, Ukraine's backing from the US is likely to be diminished under Trump. The sustainability of US arms shipments to Ukraine remains uncertain, especially now that Republicans have control of Congress.

Europe has committed to a Ukrainian victory defined by minimal territorial concessions and Kyiv's further integration into the West. Without any formal or backchannel route to the Kremlin, the EU may have to accept the terms decided by Trump, Putin and Zelensky. Trump trusts Putin and believes his plan can end the war. Still, it would not be a Trump plan without ambiguity or contradictions, which the self-declared negotiator-in-chief might justify as a means for gaining leverage. Trump may use the possibility of stopping military assistance to encourage Zelensky to negotiate, while indicating to Putin that US aid would resume if negotiations did not take place.[14] If Zelensky declined to engage with Putin, Trump would then have a reason to discontinue support for Ukraine.

The Washington Post has reported that Trump privately suggested ending the war by pressuring Ukraine to cede Crimea and the Donbas to Russia.[15] Vice President J.D. Vance has said Trump is opposed to Ukraine joining NATO, favouring neutrality instead.[16] Most Trump advisers oppose further NATO enlargement which would entail increased US responsibilities.

Negotiations among Trump, Putin and Zelensky would face challenges due to the significant differences in the objectives of Moscow and Kyiv, and the reluctance of both sides to cease hostilities. However, unsuccessful negotiations could pose difficulties for Europe. Trump might leave the Ukraine issue to Europe, requiring European decision-makers to determine how to support Ukraine in its ongoing conflict and reconstruction efforts. An American withdrawal from unproductive talks could undermine Ukrainian and European security, especially if there is a reduction in the US presence and involvement in NATO.

SECURITY DEPENDENCE

As China becomes a military rival to the United States and Washington shifts its focus towards Asia, Europe must prepare to defend itself. Europeans need to increase spending on their defence against Russia and rebuild Ukraine.

Not mincing his words, Trump has warned that Russia could 'do whatever the hell they want' with delinquent NATO members. He later said this was a 'form of negotiation' and confirmed the US would stay in NATO if Europe 'plays fair'.[17] Even if America doesn't leave NATO under Trump, its commitment to defending European NATO members against Russian aggression is less determined. Trump might reduce US funding and forces for NATO. He ordered troop withdrawals from Germany near the end of his first term, which the Biden administration later reversed. His advisers had a hard time getting him to reaffirm NATO's Article V or support collective security during his first term.

Protected by the US security umbrella, the European Union has experienced a long period of peace and is not sufficiently prepared for new threats. There are also different threat perceptions among EU member states. While some countries, such as Estonia, feel highly threatened by Russia, others, such as Portugal, Italy and Belgium, are less worried. The EU has failed to develop a strong defence capability and a common security strategy, which makes it vulnerable.

The threats of Putin's Russia and the prospect of a US pullback should compel Europe to adopt a historic paradigm shift. Forcing the Europeans to be more self-sufficient may become a godsend if it also results in a stop to their economic decline. The EU must strengthen its defence capabilities, prepare its industries and secure its supply chains. Ensuring security and its financing must become Europe's foremost priority, and it is imperative to bolster native capabilities to counter long-term military threats.

There are dangers in spending the frequently used '2 per cent' of GDP on buying American military equipment to appease Trump. This would be just as unsustainable as responding to protection rackets. Before his second inauguration, Trump already mused about '5 per cent'. Rather, by developing their own military capabilities independent of the US, in the conventional as well as in the nuclear sector, the Europeans can prevent blackmail attempts by the second Trump administration or the Russian leadership.

TRUMP THE TRIGGER

Trump's 'America First' nationalism may compel Europe to address its strategic vulnerabilities and prepare for a multipolar world. Without another Trump challenge, European leaders in Berlin and other capitals might not see any urgency to make changes. Europeans were surprised by Trump's election in 2016, viewing it as a one-off, an aberration. Yet Trump's return to the White House highlights the isolationist and populist trends in American politics. With Trump adopting a transactional approach with other powers, Europe will need to learn how to defend its interests against the US. If Trump negotiates a peace deal with Russia without considering European perspectives, it should be clear-cut evidence of Washington's new disregard for EU interests.

Yet a weak Europe does not benefit the United States in the long term. With the rise of non-Western powers in Asia and other parts of the world, a stronger Europe could be an indispensable partner. The second Trump administration might seek European support against China and other threats. The EU's experiences with multilateralism could offer valuable insights for US engagement in a multipolar world.

However, Washington must have good reasons to abandon the view that Europe is declining to appreciate its value for the US. Instead of the clearcut victory over evil and triumph of a united West, which Europeans imagined would be the outcome of Putin's invasion, Europe's future now needs to be recast. The Ukraine war has become a turning-point for whether Europe can renew itself and again become a global power.

INTERNAL COHESION

Common debt could support Europe's defence and help finance Ukraine's reconstruction, balancing social and military expenditures. Instead of using their foreign exchange reserves and savings to invest in US debt and boosting the military-industrial complex, European countries and investors could focus on strengthening their currency, security capabilities, digital infrastructure and future technologies in preparation for increased competition.

Given the vast US government debt, a deep, liquid market of safe EU bonds would offer international investors an opportunity for risk diversification. They could park their money in euro-denominated bonds instead of US Treasury bills. With a growing government deficit and rising interest rates, the US fiscal situation is becoming increasingly untenable.[18] By investing their capital reserves in the euro and strengthening Europe economically and militarily, the 'old' continent could prepare itself for a world of geopolitical competition. A strong euro not only secures the EU's ability to act economically but also the possibility of building independent foreign and security policies.

While China has clearly recognised the implications of monetary policy and is taking steps to rival the dollar as the world's reserve currency in the future, there are no corresponding attempts in Europe to develop the euro into a global reserve currency. Although the euro's share in foreign exchange reserves is increasing worldwide, there have been no initiatives to make the currency a key source of geoeconomic power.

In this new world order, characterised by geoeconomic and geopolitical risk, only European unity can provide the necessary market power and options for action ensuring the continent's self-determination. However, terms such as 'strategic independence' and 'autonomy' currently only conceal the EU's insufficient decision-making and competencies that urgently need reform.

Both US and EU leaders have struggled to grasp the significant changes of the last decade, with the latter arguably being slower to understand their magnitude. Since 2008, US protectionist policies that increased competition from China have undercut the open marketplace that Europe has relied on for its economic growth. In contrast to previous decades, when China mainly consumed German products, Chinese subsidised companies now produce high-quality, low-cost electric vehicles and compete globally.

The ambitious 'Made in China 2025' programme caused shock waves, catching US and European attention and ramping up American fears of being surpassed. With its industrial strategy China's leadership formulated the self-confident goal of achieving global market leadership in 10 value-added-intensive industrial sectors while also determining international standards.[19] Europe faces a slow decline unless it can catchup and starts competing with China and the US.

CHAPTER 3

From Chimerica to China Shock

Chimerica—the economic colossus combining China and the United States in a mutually dependent machine—is a distant memory these days. The economic Chimerica joined together Chinese export-led development with US over-consumption in the late 1990s and early 2000s and was a term that the British historian Niall Ferguson and the German economist Moritz Schularick created to describe this rare phenomenon, labelling it as a 'marriage'. According to them, China 'was able to quadruple its GDP since 2000, raise exports by a factor of five, import western technology and create tens of millions of manufacturing jobs for the rural poor'.[1] The US could outspend its national income by an estimated 45 per cent.[2] The easy credit afforded by China's purchase of US debt meant many Americans could go a spending spree, including buying houses they could not afford. The good times between the two top economies ensured the global economy benefited too. Around two-fifths of global economic growth during the 2000s was the result of frenzied activity on both sides: surging exports and overconsumption. Post-Cold War globalisation was at its height.

China's export-led growth was nothing new. West Germany and Japan did the same after World War II. But over time their currencies appreciated against the US dollar as their economies grew. China, however, pegged its currency against the US dollar along with buying US debt which Beijing saw as a cushion against financial instability that could lead to political upheaval at home.[3]

The 2007-08 financial crisis was the death knell for Chimerica. Economists don't just put the blame on China for its obsession with exports, which continues today, but also the US Federal Reserve. Its chair, Alan Greenspan, who stepped down shortly before the 2007-08 financial crisis, later apologised for having failed to spot the housing crisis and rein in the expanding credit that was offered to new house buyers.[4]

'China Shock', another term invented by economists David H. Autor, David Dorn and Gordon H. Hanson,[5] was a product of Chimerica and occurred simultaneously with it but is still in broad usage. The economists found that a total of roughly 2 million US jobs were lost, including almost a million in the manufacturing sector between 1997 and 2011 due to increased Chinese imports. The numbers—as the authors and other economists have emphasised—are not important. The displacement of workers due to Chinese imports 'amounts to a sliver of the average churn in the US labour market, where about 60 million job separations typically take place each year'.[6] The US has been losing manufacturing jobs since 1982, before China was an economic threat. What was different with 'China Shock' was that the displaced workers did not move to find new employment as had previous generations of out-of-work Americans looking for new opportunities.

Technological innovation and automation are the real threats to many workers. Manufacturing employment has been falling sharply in all high-income economies,[7] including in Japan and Germany, major manufacturing centres. China's share of manufacturing jobs also peaked at 30 per cent in 2012 and has been falling ever since.[8] But China, with its giant economy, makes up a staggering proportion of the world's manufacturing, 35 per cent in 2020. That is more than the combined output of the US (12 per cent), Japan (6), Germany (4), India (3), South Korea (3), Italy (2), France (2), and the UK (2).[9]

The 'China Shock' plateaued around 2010-12 in terms of displacing workers but as Autor, the lead author of the 2016 economic paper, has said, it has had a long afterlife in the years since.[10] It now covers all the real and supposed wrongs that the US has suffered at the hands of China.

CHINA AS SCAPEGOAT

The West is much better at pointing fingers at others than looking at itself in the mirror. Few seem to remember that the US and Europe were the big winners by far of post-Cold War globalisation, even if it greatly accelerated China's rise and displaced Western workers. Companies thrived, executive pay skyrocketed, and the top 1 per cent benefited enormously.

The Washington establishment in the early 2000s assumed China would take its place as an unofficial partner for America. In a briefing for senior US officials at the beginning of the second George W. Bush administration, we recall, there was outrage at the idea that China would not want to always be a satellite in the US orbit. For most China experts, there was a strong belief given Chimerica that Beijing would want to keep on very good terms with Washington. Barack Obama was perhaps the last US president to believe that the two countries could work together in a G-2 to deal with world problems. Already by his second term, such an idea had been thrown aside, and China was evolving into being today's enemy and No 1 competitor.

For the Washington establishment, which has forgotten Chimerica and the benefits that accrued to the US, there's now regret that China was ever allowed into the WTO with US help. One of its biggest pokes in Western eyes has been that China rose as an authoritarian state. For many development theorists, by not liberalising as it has grown wealthier, it has defied gravity.

Rising faster than any great power in history, China managed with its 1.3 billion population to become the largest economy in purchasing power parity terms in just four decades. Its economic influence has been growing rapidly in both size and reach around the world. Before 2000, America was dominating global trade,[11] with over 80 per cent of countries trading with it more than they did with China. By 2018, that number had dropped sharply to just 30 per cent, as China has taken the top position in 128 of 190 countries.[12] China has now overtaken the US as the largest trade partner to more countries than any other. For most of Latin America—in America's backyard—China is their top trading partner. China has also boosted foreign aid, rivalling and often outdoing Western sources.

While China has been engaging globally, the US has withdrawn. Since the 2007-08 financial crisis, the US has gradually closed its doors to the rest of the world. Obama had a plan to put the US at the centre of two large regional trading networks, one connecting the US to Europe in the Transatlantic Trade and Investment Partnership (TTIP), the other with Asia in the Trans-Pacific Partnership (TPP). Both the Democratic Party's progressive left and Trump killed the effort. Vermont

Senator Bernie Sanders opposed TPP in 2016 when running against Hillary Clinton, who had served under Obama and backed TPP. But to unite the party behind her, she dropped her support of TPP. Trump campaigned against TPP in 2016 and when he won, dropped it and TTIP. Biden who was Obama's vice president, never sought to revive the regional trade deals and even his Indo-Pacific Trade Framework which is an attempt to bind Asians to the US does not guarantee any market access for them. From Chimerica two decades ago, the feeling has gone to the other extreme of avoiding any dependence on other countries.

Beijing has long had the same concerns believing China is even more vulnerable to being cut off from essential trade, such as on food and energy. In a November 2018 speech and, more recently, during the closing ceremony of the 2023 National People's Congress, Xi Jinping reiterated that tensions with the US and others were forcing China to 'travel the road of self-reliance'.[13] But even before Xi's intervention, in 2013 Beijing had announced its 'Made in China 2025' programme to make China self-sufficient in tech and able to surpass the West. The programme uses government subsidies, state-owned enterprises, heightened R & D, the training of a huge cohort of scientists and engineers, plus intellectual property theft to catch up. Agriculture and energy are the other areas where there is a strong push toward self-sufficiency.

A 2024 US Federal Reserve evaluation of the 'Made in China 2025' showed that 'China has been moving towards achieving its stated goal of reducing imports' in the key areas mentioned above even though exports to Western countries remain high.[14] China has scaled up exports in sectors like autos, and exports have become more closely linked to the overall GDP growth.

Indeed, on EVs and renewable energy, China has made itself

indispensable. The West cannot meet its climate goals without help from China. The 'supply chain for renewable energy technology is even more concentrated than for fossil fuels',[15] with China refining 80 per cent of all rare-earth minerals, 95 per cent of the world's cobalt vital to produce lithium-ion batteries, making 70 per cent of silica-based solar photovoltaic modules, and possessing three-quarters of global EV battery production capacity. Thanks to lower labour costs and having more equipment manufacturers, China also builds battery factories at practically half the cost of those in the US or Europe, according to Heiner Heimes, a professor at RWTH Aachen University in Germany.[16]

While trade with the West remains important, China has been turning to the Global South not just for trading but also investment. Under Chimerica, China invested in US bonds and dollar-denominated assets, but this changed with the souring of ties. The 2013 Belt and Road Initiative was an effort to establish inland supply chains that were less vulnerable to the US ability to divert. Since 2014, BRI members have been the recipients of over 60 per cent of the investment flows and since 2020, they have received three out of every four dollars that China invests.[17]

Critics, including some inside China, charge that many of the investments have been wasteful and the investment would have earned more in US bonds. However, the infrastructure investments are as much geopolitical as economic assistance, knitting together many Global South countries with China and making them dependent on it. The money comes without the usual conditions that the World Bank or others demand and is delivered much faster. The World Bank commended the BRI 'for speed[ing] up economic development and reduc[ing] poverty for dozens of developing countries' but chided it for 'not accompany[ing] [it] by deep policy reforms that increase transparency, improve debt sustainability, and mitigate environmental, social and corruption risks'.[18] BRI is much larger than the World Bank's[19] and US[20] investments in developing states. Hence the growing influence that has resulted from developing countries' reliance on China.

CHALLENGES AND OPPORTUNITIES

Changes on the external front could make China a more powerful player in international affairs. Certainly, the US remains an Asian power because China's neighbours fear its hostile actions. In recent years, China has been throwing its weight around, becoming overtly aggressive and demanding outward respect or else. This approach hasn't worked and won't work. Beijing should understand that trying to recreate the Middle Kingdom with an array of tributary states circling China is just another form of colonialism that developing states vehemently reject.

With the US, if not the whole West, turning inward—a process that predates Trump—China has now an opportunity to fill a vacuum, creating with others a multipolar world. While the US has 'pivoted to Asia'—primarily militarily to contain China's rise—Beijing is taking advantage of Washington's strategic narrow-mindedness and making progress through trade and generous investment in making increasing numbers of countries in practically all regions dependent more on China than the US. The American co-author worked in 2021 with a team at the University of Denver to track just how expansive China's influence had become. Its report reminds us that 'Historically, economic trade—including military sales—has been an instrument for great powers to build networks of influence. The ties that begin with trade and investment have often given a boost to establishing strong political and cultural relationships'.[21]

Outside of the West, China has taken over America's and Europe's former roles. China's 'inroads' into Africa have also seen a decline in Western influence. Besides Africa, Chinese influence outweighs US influence across much of Southeast, East Asia and South America, and has increased in former Soviet states such as Central Asia, where Russia's influence has eroded. Even in the Middle East, China has been gaining a bigger economic and diplomatic footprint. By 2020, the capacity of the Chinese to exert influence had surpassed that of the US in 61 countries.[22]

CHINA'S ECONOMIC FUTURE

China's outreach, as impressive as it is, is an attempt to compensate for problems at home. The Chinese leadership focuses on boosting exports because domestic consumption is not sufficient to sustain economic growth. And there are bigger challenges ahead. The country will grow old before it gets rich. It is unlikely to reach its goal of per capita income on Western levels by the centenary of Communist rule, which started in 1949. China still has many poor and with a much lower median income, it is only the largest economic power (measured with PPP), because its population is much larger than of any Western state.

Economically, China will never be in the position of Russia. It is too vital to the global economy. The same level of sanctions imposed on Russia would bring down the global economy if applied to China. The country is still hardening itself, wanting developing countries to depend on it while striving to be more self-sufficient. For now, though, it still needs trade with Europe and the United States. Without strong export markets, deflation would be an even greater economic threat given consumers at home are leery of spending. Beijing no doubt hopes to avoid the full brunt of Trump's tariffs by negotiating a deal that eliminates a race to the bottom that would hurt China more than America.[23]

Slow economic growth going ahead could de-legitimise the Chinese Communist Party (CCP), but more likely, the West will save it. The more the West threatens China, the more the people rally around the CCP. Only if China lost a military conflict with the United States might we expect to see the party overthrown.

CHINA AND TRUMP

Trump's return may not be so upsetting for Beijing. It already likes the fact that Trump is not smitten with Taiwan, blaming the island for stealing the chip industry away from the US decades ago and warning them that they must pay for their defence just like European allies. Trump has also said he wants to sideline the hawkish neocons at home and steer clear of war, not just with China but everywhere. Yet this sentiment isn't shared by most Republicans, including his vice-president and many of his most important Cabinet secretaries.

Concern is growing that America is falling behind China in terms of technology. The patriotic mood is more about ensuring America keeps as much power as possible. The real problem for the US foreign policy elite goes beyond the fact that China has not followed the Western playbook of democratisation and liberal market reforms, but that a stronger China threatens the long-held position as No 1 held by the United States.

In his first term, Trump levied tariffs on Chinese goods ranging from 10-30 per cent. He blacklisted Huawei but then reversed the decision, allowing US companies to sell to the telecoms company. Biden has gone further against China, not only retaining the tariffs and pressuring other countries not to buy Huawei 5G technology but also cutting off exports of high-end chips and manufacturing equipment. The regulations block Chinese access to not just US firms, but all advanced chips and equipment produced anywhere with US technology. They also bar US citizens from assisting the Chinese. Trump will no doubt continue, if not expand, these restrictions.

On the Chinese side, there was anger but also confidence that whatever the barriers Washington puts up, Beijing would overcome them. 'Nothing will hold back China's fight on advancing in chip technology and tech development [...] though the fight will be arduous and last long,' maintains the Global Times, the Party's nationalist mouthpiece.[24]

Efforts to stop China's military and economic expansion have confirmed Beijing's long-held suspicions that Washington would try to stop China's rise. The increasingly punitive measures under both Trump and Biden have become a long-term trend. Xi saw this early on and, in a 2020 Politburo meeting, reportedly talked about a 'protracted war' with the United States.[25] Besides expanding the military, he has doubled down on technology development, building a more self-sufficient China, less vulnerable to US interference.

When Biden ordered curbs on tech exports, the Financial Times' Edward Luce warned that the president had 'launched a full-blown economic war on China—all but committing the US to stopping its rise' without most Americans understanding the consequences.[26] Some American commentators have equated it with Franklin D. Roosevelt's oil sanctions against Imperial Japan, which historians believe helped spark Tokyo's decision to attack Pearl Harbor on 7 December 1941.[27]

Economic conflicts have the potential to escalate into military confrontations.[28] If President Trump were to intensify economic pressures on China to such a degree that the communist country perceives it as a stranglehold, Beijing might respond with measures such as a blockade of Taiwan. The island is at the core of Sino-US rivalry—not only geographically, but also in chip manufacturing, a cutting-edge industry that many believe will decide economic and military superiority in the future.

Beijing's rhetoric and actions are no less bellicose. A decades-long Chinese military build-up, including the rapid growth of its arsenal of nuclear weapons, worries security experts across the political spectrum in the US. While capabilities should not be confused with intentions, China's behaviour in the South China Sea and towards American allies in the region has not assuaged the concerns of US strategic planners. China has ramped up its military exercises off Taiwan, which look increasingly like rehearsals for an invasion.

These moves reinforce America's bleak assessment of China's strategic intention to drive it out of the Western Pacific. Elbridge Colby, Trump's nominee for the No 3 position at the Pentagon,[29] will raise fears in Beijing and elsewhere that Trump is prepared to confront China's aggressive activities. Colby has argued for redeploying US military assets away from Europe and Middle East to the Pacific. He believes war is inevitable if the US wants to remain the predominant power.

Besides worries that the population would blame them for any failure, Chinese leaders are not confident of winning such a contest, at least in the next few years. They see more advantage in trying to intimidate the people of Taiwan into submission and it may be working. Looking at Ukraine and the devastation it has suffered, Taiwanese might prefer to avoid conflict with China. Most polling indicates they would prefer no change in status, even if they like the idea of independence.[30]

'The business of America is business', a statement attributed to President Calvin Coolidge, could also summarise Trump's foreign policy preferences. The big question is whether Trump can keep his anti-China appointees in line if there is a crisis. Competing with China will involve addressing its growing presence in the Middle East.

CHAPTER 4

Rebalancing the Middle East

Stephen Cook, an analyst at the Council on Foreign Relations, offers a comprehensive view of US involvement in the Middle East from the Cold War to recent times.[1] Initially focused on securing oil supplies, ensuring Israel's safety, and countering Soviet influence, US policymakers saw their Cold War victory as a chance to promote peace and democracy in the region. This led to several missteps, notably George W. Bush's disastrous invasion of Iraq, Trump's exit from the Iran deal, and Biden's misjudgment before the October 7 attack on Israel (when his administration declared 'the region is quieter than it has been for decades').[2] For the future, Cook advises caution and balance for US foreign policy. However, both with conflicts in the Middle East and the potential for de-dollarisation as the Gulf energy markets shift towards Asia, Trump has little political will and few tools to resolve the underlying issues. By staying out and not wanting to act as a regional policeman in coordination with other powers, the chances for any permanent peace are limited.

Israel's punitive attacks in Gaza have swung global opinion to the Palestinians as well as their supporters like Russia and China, who are strengthening their ties with Tehran. With Israel's widening of the war to Lebanon and the land grab in Syria, the decline of US influence in Israel since the October 7 attack has been notable. While Israel's military might abide by the ceasefire terms and halt its attacks, Netanyahu appears to be planning for continued military oversight of Gaza. A lasting peace remains elusive as long as the Palestine question is unresolved.

Only the United States can strong-arm Israel into accepting a two-state solution. The Israeli settlements remain a big obstacle, making a cohesive Palestinian entity on the West Bank impossible, while Gaza's future is highly uncertain. In the event of a Palestinian state, the Israeli settlers would feel surrounded and are likely to start a civil war to protect their future. Partial or full annexation of the West Bank and Gaza, which some hardliners in the Netanyahu government would like, could be the next shoe to drop, making Israel an international pariah, without support anywhere, except in Trump's government.

IRAN'S AMBITIONS

Iran's possible development of nuclear weapons will be the next big crisis, potentially causing a US–Israeli showdown with Iran. Israel fears that Iran could use nuclear weapons as a deterrent, serving as a 'nuclear shield' for it to pursue its objectives more aggressively without fear of retaliation. Currently, Iran can't afford to risk escalation. With Hamas and Hezbollah weakened and Assad driven from Damascus, Tehran has suffered a loss of allies and supporters.

Iranian officials have suggested that Israel's aggressive stance might lead Iran to complete its nuclear weapons development.[3] Iran's Supreme Leader Ayatollah Ali Khamenei may revoke his previous fatwa banning nuclear weapons. In April 2024, Rafael Grossi, head of the International Atomic Energy Agency (IAEA), reported that Iran has been enriching uranium to 60 per cent purity, much higher than the typical 2 to 4 per cent of other nuclear powers and close to weapons-grade. Grossi stated that while Iran has enough nuclear material for several warheads, it did not yet have a nuclear weapon, though the situation remains serious. He also noted that the IAEA's inspection level was inadequate.[4]

America and Israel have consistently affirmed their opposition to Iran developing a nuclear bomb. Israel is believed to have accurate intelligence on Iran's nuclear programme. If Iran crosses a critical line, Israel might attack its nuclear facilities, as it nearly did in 2011.[5] However, it is uncertain if Jerusalem could fully destroy all nuclear sites, and such an attack might prompt Iran to hasten the production of a nuclear weapon.

During the election campaign, the Biden administration played down concerns about Iran's nuclear activities and even pushed European allies not to rebuke Iran over its nuclear programme at an IAEA meeting.[6] Nor did Tehran want to promote Trump's election victory by escalating the conflict after Israel's measured response on 26 October 2024 to Iran's firing of over 180 missiles on 1 October 2024, which was in retaliation for the Israeli assassination of Hezbollah secretary-general Hassan Nasrallah and Hamas leader Ismail Haniyeh.

Sanctions have primarily benefited Russia and China. Moscow has strengthened military ties with Tehran, while China enjoys cheap Iranian oil that Europe and America's Asian allies are no longer allowed to buy. Despite this cooperation, Iran cannot rely on Russia or China to defend itself if the second Trump administration pursues regime change.

RUSSIA'S INTERESTS

Putin has enhanced Russia's military collabouration with Iran and had supported the now defunct Assad regime in Syria alongside Iran. The collapse of Assad is a blow to Russian influence unless Moscow manages to keep its airbase in Northwest Syria and a naval facility at Tartus. The airbase is used as a staging post for military contractors flying to Africa. In a promising sign for Moscow, the new Hayat Tahrir al-Sham's (HTS)-dominated Syrian Salvation government did not allow the ransacking of the Russian embassy in Damascus, as was the case for the Iranian mission. Most of the weaponry in the Syrian arsenal is Soviet or Russian made, and the new government will need Moscow's help to maintain it.

Iran primarily uses domestically produced weapons but also purchases some from Russia. For its part, Iran has provided Russia with drone technology during its operations in Ukraine. Iran has also supplied Fath 360 short-range missiles and trained Russians in their use.[7] These missiles enable Russia to reserve its advanced long-range missiles for other purposes in Ukraine. US security agencies anticipate more arms sales and closer military cooperation between the two.

Trump may demand concessions from Russia regarding Iran, while giving in to Russian territorial demands in Ukraine, which he has already signaled.[8] In return for Russia staying out of a US-led attack on Iran, Trump could accede to Russian claims over Crimea and the Donbas. However, Putin may not go along as Russia would appear complicit and risk undoing the strong military ties it has built with Iran.

OPPORTUNITY FOR CHINA

Amid rising tensions with Israel, Beijing expressed support for Tehran, though their relationship is largely commercial as Iran is unlikely to involve Beijing in a distant conflict. Iran has no leverage; on the contrary, Tehran is dependent on China. Iran relies heavily on its energy trade with China, with more than 90 per cent of its crude oil exports sold there through unofficial channels.[9] In 2021, the two countries entered a 25-year agreement wherein China committed to making significant investments to secure its oil supply.[10] If Israel targets and destroys Iran's oil infrastructure, Beijing will likely pledge to rebuild it.

China supports Iran diplomatically and opposes US policies, but it shows limited interest in a security role in the Middle East. While US security agencies are concerned about an alleged 'axis of anger',[11] China's support for Iran, like its support for Russia in Ukraine, is pragmatic and limited.

China also faces the challenge of balancing its relations with Israel. For decades, China and Israel have had a productive technological partnership, which grew during the Israeli tech boom in 2000s. In confidential talks, US officials have expressed their concerns about this cooperation and tried to dissuade Israel from it.

China is taking steps to position itself as a counterbalance to the United States in the Gulf region. In March 2023, Beijing facilitated a reconciliation between long-time rivals Saudi Arabia and Iran. Analysts in Washington noted these developments with keen interest, considering the impact on the US close alliance with Riyadh from Saudi Arabia aligning more closely with Beijing.

SAUDI ARABIA'S OIL POWER

Since President Franklin D. Roosevelt met King Abdulaziz bin Abdul Rahman Al Saud on the USS Quincy on 14 February 1945, the US–Saudi relationship has been one of the most important geopolitical alliances. The 'security for oil' deal offered US protection in exchange for stable oil prices from Saudi Arabia. However, due to America achieving energy independence via fracking, Saudi leaders now doubt US reliability.

International oil prices are still influenced by OPEC and in crises like the Iran–Israel conflict. Saudi Arabia remains the only 'swing producer' capable of noticeably influencing oil prices through its production behaviour. This explains why Biden travelled to Riyadh in July 2022 to seek cooperation from Saudi Crown Prince Mohammed Bin Salman, despite having previously labelled him a 'pariah'.[12] His efforts were unsuccessful; Saudi Arabia did not increase oil production. Instead, in October 2022, OPEC decided to cut supplies by two million barrels per day, raising oil prices.[13]

Trump's policies aim to increase domestic oil production and reduce regulatory hurdles to lower energy prices. To reduce gasoline prices in the long-term, however, Trump will also be dependent on Saudi Arabia. Unlike Biden, Trump has maintained close relations with Saudi Arabia. During his first term, he strongly supported Saudi Arabia and took a hard line against its arch enemy Iran. He also stood behind the crown prince after the murder of the Washington Post columnist Jamal Khashoggi. Trump's pragmatism paid off; evidenced when he successfully worked with Saudi Arabia and Russia to reduce oil production and stabilised prices in the wake of the slump in demand caused by the Covid-19 pandemic. This collabouration was crucial to supporting the US oil industry.

In his second term, Trump could try to make similar agreements, this time, to lower gasoline prices. However, this won't be an easy task as global oil prices are affected by many factors, including worldwide demand and geopolitical tensions. If, for example, the conflict between Israel and Iran escalates and Iran blocks the Strait of Hormuz, which is important for oil deliveries, oil prices would rise significantly.

CHALLENGES AHEAD

Trump's previous strategy of fostering peace through economic ties between Israel and Arab states, along with applying maximum pressure on Iran, faces challenges as both Russia and China have strengthened their relations with Tehran. The second Trump administration will also face the challenge of addressing Middle East stability or risk broader conflicts due to Israel's dominance.

Should Israel, emboldened by Trump's assurance that he would not hold back Netanyahu, take the preemptive step of bombing nuclear sites, prompting a retaliation from Iran, Trump may feel compelled to intervene militarily. Trump aims to strengthen ties with both Israel and Saudi Arabia, while taking a tougher stance on Iran. Yet isolating Iran will deepen its reliance on Russia and China, enhancing the latters' influence. Balancing power in the Middle East will test US capability to thrive in a multipolar world.

The creation of OPEC+ (Saudi-led OPEC plus Russia) in 2016 marked a significant turning point in global oil dynamics and ushered in a new era of cooperation between Saudi Arabia and Russia. A key catalyst for this cooperation was Russia's annexation of Crimea in 2014 and the ensuing conflict in

Donbas. Since the agreement was signed, OPEC+ has operated effectively without much distinction between OPEC and non-OPEC members, with Saudi Arabia and Russia playing a crucial role in the discussions.

These discussions are of concern to strategists in Washington because the source of American power is at stake. The petrodollar system, where Saudi Arabia prices its oil in US dollars, has supported US financial dominance for decades.

Saudi Arabia has been considering pricing oil in other currencies, potentially weakening the greenback's dominance. This is part of Saudi Arabia's broader strategy to diversify its economy and enhance regional security. Moving away from the petrodollar could impact global trade and financial stability, but, for now, the US dollar remains central due to the Saudi riyal's fixed exchange rate and dollar reserves.

CHAPTER 5

Global South Left Out

The Global South spans the vast middle belt of the world from Latin America, Africa, the Middle East, South and Southeast Asia and has become a replacement term for the 'Third World' to describe low- to middle-income developing countries. Many Global South countries have become middle powers[1] and the more prosperous ones among them—a category designated as emerging markets—will see faster per capita GDP growth than the United States in the next decade. Unlike the US, they are in a more sustainable fiscal position having far lower budgets and account deficits, allowing more room for growth-driving investments.[2] For the IMF, G20 emerging markets 'have doubled their share of world trade and foreign direct investment and now account for one-third of global GDP'.[3] However, other middle powers not a part of the G20 emerging markets, such as Nigeria and Pakistan, are suffering the plight of the poorer developing states. While important geopolitically, Nigeria and Pakistan are in danger of becoming failed states requiring more global attention.

So far we have not detected any use of the term Global South by Trump or other close political associates. Global South or the Global Majority, as some of its citizens call it, gained currency during the Ukraine war. Assuming the Global South countries, most of which were former colonies, would see Russia's invasion of Ukraine as a holdover from the colonialist past, the West was shocked when many condemned Russia's actions but wanted no part in economically or diplomatically isolating Moscow. For many developing countries, their alienation can be traced to the West's disregard for their struggle with the Covid-19 pandemic,[4] if not further back.

Additionally, many middle-power states like India, Indonesia and Brazil have eschewed 'naming and shaming' values-based diplomacy, seeing such moralising as a danger to their wish for multiple alignments across the West, China and Russia. Many are closely integrated with China on trade and investments—on which their economic growth depends—but East Asians particularly have sought to remain under the US security umbrella protecting against Beijing's increasing assertiveness. There is a schizophrenic pattern in Asia and the Middle East, where middle-powers lean toward China, their largest trading partner, on economic issues but look to the US on security. Pushed to choose between Pax Americana and the business opportunities offered by China, even US partners prefer 'all of the above'. Michael Singh, a former senior director for Middle East affairs at the US National Security Council, draws attention to the 'new global reality' Washington should reckon with: 'By and large, it is neither the United States nor China they see as most threatening, but the competition between them'.[5]

POWER VACUUM

Many Global South countries distrust multilateral bodies like the UN Security Council or the Bretton Woods institutions because they see them as monopolised by or too beholden to the great powers. The Biden administration conceded that the World Bank should have been more active in helping developing countries deal with climate change. It's highly unlikely under Trump that they will get a better hearing.

Until the Global South obtains more leadership positions in multilateral institutions, their legitimacy in the eyes of middle-power governments will continue to decline. The United States has the final say in appointing the president of the World Bank, which is usually an American, and Trump's appointee during his first term, David Malpass, a climate change sceptic, faced strong criticism for not funneling more assistance to help poor countries deal with climate issues. Current President Ajay Banga was appointed by Biden in 2023 and would likely serve four to five years, giving the second Trump administration another shot at choosing the top person.

Other multilateral institutions like the UN Security Council or IMF are frozen in time. The Biden administration proposed an expansion of the UN Security Council, but the new permanent members would lack the veto, making them into second-class world citizens. It's unlikely the Trump administration would even go as far in trying to devise a scheme to expand the Security Council. On the IMF, the Europeans so far have insisted on their prerogative to appoint the head, currently an economist from Bulgaria. The G-7 nations, for example, have 59 per cent of IMF voting rights with only 14 per cent of the world's population.

The BRICS expansion that Putin and Xi oversaw could make it an alternative to Western-dominated institutions. The expanded BRICS, which include founders Brazil, Russia, India, China and South Africa, plus four new members, one of which is the United Arab Emirates, and 13 partner countries, all of whom have been actively discussing ways to reduce their reliance on the US dollar and challenge its dominance in the global economy. In their 'de-dollarisation' efforts, the BRICS nations have been exploring various strategies, such as developing their own currency for international trade and creating alternative financial systems that do not depend on the dollar.

Trump takes these developments seriously and threatened participating countries with 100 per cent tariffs if they continued to undermine the dollar. 'The idea that the BRICS Countries are trying to move away from the Dollar while we stand by and watch is OVER. We require a commitment from these Countries that they will neither create a new BRICS Currency, nor back any other Currency to replace the mighty US Dollar or, they will face 100% Tariffs and should expect to say goodbye to selling into the wonderful US Economy. They can go find another sucker!', Trump wrote on 1 December 2024 on X.[6]

BRICS Pay has more potential than a new currency to rival the bank messaging network of the Society for Worldwide Interbank Financial Telecommunication (SWIFT). Russia's Mir network, India's Unified Payment Interface and China's WePay and Alipay would all serve as strong foundations to create BRICS Pay and allow participating countries to trade in their own currency, not the dollar.[7] Russia was surprised by the support it received at the 2024 Kazan summit from other BRICS countries to develop this idea.

Western commentators have largely seen BRICS as a Russian and Chinese publicity stunt, but a broader swath of middle powers, not just the BRICS, are reducing their dollar holdings and diversifying their reserve currencies. They are also buying gold, which one Western economist has warned is an increasingly persistent trend, signalling growing distrust of US management of the global financial system[8] and increasing interest in alternatives to the dollar-based financial system. However, dethroning the dollar will be a long and challenging journey. The dollar remains the benchmark for global commodities and holds a significant share of global foreign exchange reserves. The BRICS countries are not a coherent economic or political bloc, and their economies and political systems vary widely, which makes it difficult for them to present a united front. Still, BRICS+ provides an alternative for countries in the Global South to access development finance, increase trade and attract investment. Moreover, it is a way to address the inequalities within the current multilateral system, which has often failed to deliver comprehensive solutions to global issues.

A DOUBLE-EDGED SWORD

The bigger threat to the dollar comes from US policymakers who have weaponised it. Both Democrats and Republicans are responsible, sanctioning or raising tariffs on countries or individuals who don't tow the US and Western line. Biden has increased the number of sanctions, more than Trump in his first term, largely due to the Ukraine War.[9] Russia and Russian individuals are the primary targets of sanctions, leading in the number imposed. The US also enforces secondary sanctions against economic activities and entities in other countries that engage in the trade of arms or dual-use technologies with adversaries of America. Iran, China, North Korea and Syria are the biggest targets for secondary sanctions. It will almost certainly continue to expand under Trump 2.0.

The US weaponization took a qualitative leap after Western powers froze and may confiscate the $260-300 billion in Russian ruble reserves that were held in the West. There has been a recent G7-EU decision to 'lend' roughly $50 billion in interest earnings to Ukraine, which for many in the Global South looks like highway robbery.

For the United States, sanctions are often the last weapon left. American military interventions are too costly and unpopular in most cases. Economic sanctions barely touch Americans. In Western media there is little evidence of a growing distaste for their use. However, study after study in the West has shown their ineffectiveness. In the US case, there is no real mechanism for lifting them even when the country or actor has stopped the sanctioned activity. Proponents will say that is a good thing as it terrorises others against getting involved in the sanctioned activity, but it also builds up resentments.

A NEW COLD WAR

The different alignments—often due to sanctions—are bringing together countries that otherwise might not have cooperated with one another. The BRICS formation was originally modeled on the Goldman Sachs analysis of the most rapidly growing emerging nations in 2001. Much has changed since then, particularly the fact that many of them are not growing economically as quickly. Given the diverse membership, it is unlikely that BRICS or similar groups will form formal alliances, despite their shared opposition to US sanctions and potential role in financial reform during a dollar crisis.

Washington, however, hopes that the various alignments it is fostering across South and Southeast Asia will become formal alliances or networks against China. Then Assistant Secretary of Defence for Indo-Pacific Affairs, Ely Ratner, has explicitly stated that the United States, with its two treaty allies (Japan and South Korea), as well as others such as Australia and India in the Quadrilateral Security Dialogue, is aiming for diversified mutual military access to allow for rapid power projection in case China invades Taiwan.[10] The Biden administration also wanted a networked security architecture to reinforce US interests and values and increase allied and partner capabilities that strengthen deterrence while lowering costs for Washington.

Digging deeper, researchers Kelly Grieco and Jennifer Kavanagh have found that achieving progress toward these goals has been slow. In a Foreign Affairs article, they state that 'three years in, the United States still lacks the military access needed for a distributed force posture, its region-wide security architecture remains ill-suited to mobilising a collective response to Chinese aggression, and its allies and partners continue to underinvest in their own defence'.[11] It is conceivable but not inevitable that this broad US-led alignment could develop into an alliance should China decide to invade Taiwan. But all Asian countries depend on trade and investment from China and therefore do not want to antagonise Beijing; thus, siding openly with Washington could have severe domestic consequences for them.

The transactional nature of the Sino-Russian-North Korea-Iran links is also important. Both China and Russia are fearful and distrustful of North Korea. Military cooperation between Russia and North Korea is based on Moscow's needs for arms in its war against Ukraine. For its part, China fears that a burgeoning Moscow-Pyongyang partnership will reduce its influence over North Korea, a longtime client. In the Middle East, China, a leading importer of both Saudi and Iranian oil, is careful to balance its ties to Iran with those to the Saudis and the broader Gulf Cooperation Council.

Sino-Russian relations have a long history of distrust and conflict. The current affinity is largely driven by mutual opposition to a US-led order. Under Putin, Moscow has accepted being the junior partner, but another Russian president might well object to what is an increasingly lopsided alliance. Isolated from the West and with much of its trade crippled, Russia's burgeoning economic ties with China are based on the latter's need for the former's oil and gas as well as other natural resources. Absent an easing of sanctions, Russia must rely on China for new investment in its energy infrastructure; so far, China has been driving a hard bargain, partly owing to fear of becoming too reliant on Russian energy.[12] The Russia–Ukraine War, as well as Russia's economic isolation, has provided an opening for the renminbi-based provision of consumer goods such as autos, grain and textiles. Yet China's integration into the global trade and financial system, and still-thick ties with the US, complicate the strategic triangle from Russia's perspective.

In both cases—America's growing ties to Asia and a stronger Russo–China friendship—the status quo is not unalterable. Loose alignments could be forged into what now appears to be an 'unthinkable' alliance.

The United States had close ties with Britain in the interwar period, but there was no guarantee that Washington would come to the aid of Britain in the event of a Nazi attack. President Franklin D. Roosevelt struggled to sell the US–UK Lend-Lease programme to an isolationist Congress and public. Only the Japanese surprise attack on Pearl Harbor brought the US into a wartime alliance with Britain and the Soviet Union. The alliance with Britain expanded into a broader Atlantic Alliance after the war, while ties with the Soviet Union were broken.

The Global South's many middle-powers such as Brazil, the Gulf states or Indonesia have grown in importance as bilateral tensions have increased between the United States and China and NATO and Russia. But the desire of most middle-powers is to be multi-aligned, that is, not taking one side but dealing with all sides. In doing so, they may be staving off a global Cold War and their lack of alignment with either side—the West or Russia and China—might help avert an outright great power conflict.

III.

CHAPTER 6

War: No Longer Unthinkable

A major war may be imminent after 75 years of peace. The United States and China are likely adversaries, with Taiwan being a potential trigger. For both nations, controlling Taiwan has become crucial. Such a conflict could involve Russia, Iran and North Korea supporting China, while Europe, Japan, Australia, Canada and others would back the United States.

The latest war games run by Washington-based think tanks show the US could stop a Chinese invasion but at great cost.[1] War gaming inside and outside the government should be a deterrent to actual conflict, particularly as the US would not come out unscathed. Former Air Force General Mark D. Kelly said that China's forces are 'designed to inflict more casualties in the first 30 hours of combat than we've endured over the last 30 years in the Middle East.'[2]

At a Washington think tank, the Centre for Strategic and International Studies, the war gaming saw the US swiftly losing 'two aircraft carriers, each carrying at least 5,000 people, on top of hundreds of aircraft, according to reports'.[3] One of the players said that however much the wargames varied, 'what almost never changes is [that] it's a bloody mess and both sides take some terrible losses'.[4] In another think tank's version, a 2022 war game ended with China detonating a nuclear weapon near Hawaii. 'Before they knew it', both Washington and Beijing 'had crossed key red lines, but neither was willing to back down', the conveners concluded.[5] In such an existential contest, there's no guarantee it wouldn't graduate to a nuclear war if one or the other side were losing.

Putin's threats to use short-range nuclear weapons in Ukraine along with US strategists advocating use of tactical nuclear weapons in a war against China risk reducing the threshold for employing nuclear weapons. Emerging technologies—AI, offensive cyber and anti-satellite weapons—are creating new vulnerabilities for nuclear powers, shrinking decision times and stoking fears of first strikes—while arms control efforts seem far off.

Even if one side or the other prevails initially, it's likely to evolve into a continual conflict as happened in the Napoleonic wars. In such titanic struggles, all sides may come out as losers, like Europe after the First World War when power shifted to America. Is America going to repeat Britain's mistake in the 1930s and retreat behind a new 'Imperial Preference'—to which London resorted in trying to enhance internal trade inside the worldwide British Empire to counter the rising economic powers, the US and Germany? 'Imperial Preference' did little to stem Britain's decline. Even before the interwar period, during the lead up to the First World War, Britain's declining power was confronted by the German Empire's aspirations, leading to what the diplomat George Kennan called Europe's 'Ur-Katastrophe', 'the great seminal catastrophe of this century', laying the groundwork for another even more bloody conflict, the Second World War.

WAR AND PEACE

Historians have noted parallels between today and the era before World War I. Margaret MacMillan, the author of The War That Ended Peace,[6] observed similarities between the 70 years since 1945—during which major powers avoided direct conflict—and the long peace after the Napoleonic wars. This period saw the growth of international law, leading Europeans to believe they had moved beyond large-scale war. MacMillan argues that this 'long peace' created the illusion that major wars were a thing of the past due to global interdependence.[7]

Anglo-German rivalry before 1914 mirrors current Sino–US competition. Britain felt threatened by Germany's encroachment on markets and power. A British pamphlet, 'Made in Germany', highlighted this threat as early as 1896, portraying Germany as a rising commercial state aiming to challenge British prosperity. Similarly, Germans believed they deserved global dominance—wishing for an empire on which the sun would never set—but saw Britain as an obstacle. Replacing Britain with the US, Germany with China, and colonies with allies describes the current geopolitical scenario.[8]

Ukraine, and increasingly Taiwan, are now considered part of the West. MacMillan observed a similar pattern before World War I, with powerful nations protecting their client states. Modern terms may differ, but the concept remains: patron nations avoid abandoning their clients to maintain an image of strength. Before 1914, great powers spoke of honour; today, US officials refer to credibility or prestige.

Although Trump claims to want to avoid another war, history shows that good intentions alone are insufficient. Taiwan's importance to the US has arguably grown, even though past presidents like Eisenhower threatened nuclear weapons against China, and Clinton mobilised naval assets in response to Chinese missile tests near Taiwan. At those times, China did not have the economic power or the blue-water navy it has today.

Cooler heads hoped to end the costly naval race before World War I, but public opinion in both Germany and Britain favoured hostility over friendship. Even the royal families' blood ties worsened rather than eased these tensions. Replace the estranged German and British royals with multilateral corporations now discouraged from doing business between the US and China, and MacMillan's description fits the growing Cold War mentality in today's world, dampening discussions of cooperation or shared interests.

Then as now, the international confrontation also stems from domestic upheaval and loss. Before 1914, European landowners faced declining prosperity due to cheap imports, a rising middle class and an emerging urban plutocracy. Consequently, many upper classes supported conservative or reactionary movements. Similarly, artisans and shopkeepers affected by changing economies leaned towards radical right-wing movements. Anti-Semitism grew as Jews were blamed for capitalism and modernity. Today, radical right-wing and populist movements in the US and Europe offer an outlet for people's frustrations and fears as changes affect their jobs and security.[9]

In modern China, the Communist Party's legitimacy hinges in part on its promise to keep raising living standards. With Xi's increasing emphasis on security, rather than just economic development, Taiwan has become a red line. For the Party and most of the Chinese public, reunification of Taiwan is the final step in undoing the 'century of humiliation' that has become the supreme duty for any Chinese leader.

TWO WOUNDED GIANTS

The United States and China are both caught up in a cycle of increasing nationalism, making it harder for either side to make concessions. They are both, in a way, wounded giants. For the US, it is that the American Dream is slipping away for most. For Chinese leaders, the increasing worry is that they will never raise their country to Western levels of prosperity.

As mentioned, China may well get old before it gets rich. It faces demographic and economic challenges as its population ages rapidly. It has already entered a period of lower growth and may get caught in the 'middle-income trap' unless it changes its statist approach. The middle-income trap refers to a situation where a country, after reaching a certain level of income, struggles to progress to high-income status. The slowdown in upward mobility for the middle class could undermine the legitimacy of the CCP.

Might Xi divert attention from domestic problems by launching an invasion of Taiwan? What would such a war look like? The common Western belief is that it would begin with a sea invasion. However, China has limited amphibious lift capability and may use non-military means to coerce Taiwan instead. A military assault might happen but is unlikely before the end of this decade.

Nonetheless, China has increasingly used military actions to wage psychological warfare against Taiwan. China's incursions into the Taiwanese air defence identification zone increased from about 20 flights in 2019 to almost 900 two years later.[10]

In the spirit of strategist Sun Tzu, China has also begun the battle to reclaim Taiwan without the use of the military. Beijing could deploy economic coercion to isolate the island. An academic study identifies several 'grey zone' measures which could involve the termination of trade, the proliferation of propaganda to reduce Taiwan's resistance to reunification through economic incentives, and heightened efforts to attract away leading talent in key sectors such as processor chip manufacturing.[11]

China has other options besides a frontal invasion. A blockade could have enormous economic repercussions. To rally international support for deterring China, the US State Department shared a forecast commissioned from US research firm the Rhodium Group that estimates a Chinese blockade of Taiwan would cost $2.5 trillion in annual global losses.[12]

THE CHIPS ARE DOWN

Due to its advanced semiconductor manufacturing—as well as its geographical location—Taiwan is at the centre of competition between China and the US. Tech competition is at the heart of the Sino-American conflict; above all, chip technologies are considered crucial for future economic and military superiority. Emerging technologies—artificial intelligence, robotics, big data, biotechnology, 3D printing, the Internet of Things—will be drivers of economic growth and military strength, and all require the latest chips.

China is more vulnerable than the US as it relies heavily on food and energy imports, making sea routes crucial. Its bond with Russia helps secure overland energy supplies, but a blockade of the Malacca Straits by the US and its allies is a major concern for Beijing. This vulnerability drives China's naval expansion, escalating tensions with the US.

In the US, the prevailing opinion is that China will avoid conflict because of its economic problems. It is often ignored that Xi could distract from the country's problems with nationalist rhetoric. Some in China's elite even believe that a crisis like the Cuban Missile Crisis could lead Washington to take China's interests more seriously. Former Australian Prime Minister Kevin Rudd cited that crisis as a precedent for how the US and China relationship could avoid collision.[13] The US and USSR came close—closer according to recent revelations than previously known—to nuclear war but in pulling back from the brink they sought to build in brakes to a future conflict with a direct hotline between the White House and Kremlin and later under the US presidents Nixon and Ford backing détente.

THE THIN LINE

For the moment, neither side wants a war over Taiwan. China is arming and biding its time. The US under Trump will be too consumed with 'Making America Great Again' and trying to isolate China economically, but a problem with the Cold War psychology is that the line separating economic sanctions from open conflict is a thin one. What is the dividing line between a cold and hot war?

During the Cuban Missile Crisis, President Kennedy received advice from Dean Acheson, the doyen of American post-World War II diplomacy, to bomb the Soviet missile sites on Cuba. Acheson later admitted that this might well have prompted retaliation from Moscow. Fortunately, Kennedy had read Barbara Tuchman's The Guns of August about the First

World War, published just months before the 1962 crisis.[14] In his memoir Swords and Ploughshares, General Maxwell Taylor recalled how the book came up during his discussions with the president:

> An avid reader of history, Kennedy has been greatly impressed by Barbara Tuchman's The Guns of August, which he often quoted as evidence that the generals are inclined to have a single solution in a crisis and thus tie the hands of the political leaders by leaving them with the choice between doing nothing and accepting an inflexible war plan. As he read Tuchman's book, it was the rigidity of the mobilization plans both of the Triple Alliance and of the Triple Entente which made it impossible for the diplomats to avert a world war in 1914. [...] In the midst of the crisis, he told his brother Bobby: 'I am not going to follow a course which will allow anyone to write a comparable book about this time [and call it] The Missiles of October.[15]

Today's warning is not to assume a conflict over Taiwan will end there. 'Neither Beijing nor Washington would accept defeat in a limited engagement,' Michael O'Hanlon, a military expert at the Brookings Institution, warns, 'Instead, the conflict probably would expand horizontally to other regions and vertically, perhaps even to include nuclear weapons threats—or their actual use. It literally could become the worst catastrophe in the history of warfare.'[16]

While a conflict over Taiwan might begin conventionally, it could quickly escalate. China's mainland bases could become US targets, prompting China to strike US islands and military facilities in the Asia-Pacific. In a prolonged conflict, Japan may face Chinese missile and bombing attacks, heightening pressure on both sides, the US and China, to consider nuclear options.

Neither Washington nor Beijing could lose without significant repercussions. A defeat for China would destabilise its leadership and fuel nationalistic demands for retribution, while no leader could accept American dominance in the Pacific again. For the US, a loss would undermine its global power and credibility as an ally protector. But even if the West was victorious in a non-nuclear confrontation, such a cold war would be devastating, not least because it would divert resources and attention from the global climate crisis—another vital threat.

CHAPTER 7

Environmental Calamity: A Virtual Certainty

Earth is likely to cross a critical threshold for global warming within the next decade, and nations will need to make an immediate and drastic shift away from fossil fuels to prevent the planet from overheating. The EU's Copernicus Climate Change Service reported 2024 was the warmest year to date and the first year above 1.5°C.[1] Each of the past four decades has been warmer than the previous one.[2]

Even more concerning is the possibility of tipping points which the Earth may cross in the next few years. The collapse of ice sheets in Greenland and the West Antarctic, the widespread thawing of permafrost, the death of coral reefs in warm waters and the collapse of an oceanic current in the North Atlantic are all possibilities.

The melting of the Greenland ice sheet is already contributing to global sea-level rise. A recent study found that Greenland's melting ice will cause at least 10 inches of sea-level rise, even if we stop emitting greenhouse gases today.[3] The West Antarctic Ice Sheet is also at risk of collapse, which could lead to several feet of sea-level rise. This would have devastating impacts on coastal communities worldwide.

Thawing permafrost in regions like Siberia and Alaska is causing the ground to sink, forming thermokarst lakes—a type of terrain characterised by very irregular surfaces of marshy hollows and small hummocks formed when ice-rich permafrost thaws—and releases large amounts of methane, a potent greenhouse gas. This accelerates climate change and disrupts local ecosystems and infrastructure.

The Great Barrier Reef has experienced multiple mass bleaching events due to rising ocean temperatures. These events have led to significant coral death, threatening marine biodiversity and the livelihoods of communities dependent on reef tourism and fishing.

The Atlantic Meridional Overturning Circulation, which includes the Gulf Stream, is showing signs of weakening. A collapse could lead to drastic cooling in northern Europe, disrupt weather patterns and have severe global climate impacts.

These changes are not reversible. There may be an upside, though. The problems the West has with China may disappear. New technologies such as AI and quantum computing may allow us to peer deeper into the mysteries of meteorology. Seriously tackling climate change will mean a revolution in lifestyles everywhere and, unlike in the pandemic, when the West could wall itself off with its effective vaccines, climate change respects no borders and fighting it requires a united effort.

Combating climate change requires worldwide cooperation; failure affects everyone. In particular, the poorest nations, which contribute least to climate change, are the most at risk. Some 54 countries, representing over half of the world's poorest population, need immediate debt relief to prevent extreme poverty and address climate change.[4] According to UN Secretary-General António Guterres, at least 107 developing countries, home to 1.7 billion people, are currently facing crises related to food, energy, or finance.[5]

At the onset of the Biden administration, Washington attempted to separate climate change discussions from other issues with Beijing, seeking cooperation on climate change while opposing various other actions or requests from China. China considered it a bad deal without the US 'respecting' China as a sovereign equal. In their late 2022 summit, Xi and Biden found a way to reinstate climate change talks. But three months following the summit, Biden's climate envoy John Kerry informed the media that progress on climate cooperation had come to a halt: '... they've kind of pulled back a little bit, expressing the feeling that all we're doing is bashing them and bashing them'.[6] Nevertheless, after a short hiatus, 'agreements between them created the basis for important successes in negotiations, such as the renewable energy targets at COP28 [Dubai, November 2023] and progress in dealing with non-CO2 greenhouse gases like methane'.[7]

Unfortunately, prospects for continued US-China cooperation on climate change look dim with an uninterested second Trump administration. There will be even more 'China bashing' with far less focus on climate issues and the need for cooperation but the dangers of climate change will intensify.

The frequency and scale of extreme weather events will increase. A global catastrophe would make competition irrelevant. Melting Arctic ice could weaken the Northern polar jet stream, disrupting weather patterns. This has already caused slower-moving high- and low-pressure systems, extending heat waves and storms that cause severe floods. Examples include the

2021 heat wave in the American West, which worsened droughts and set record temperatures, the 2022 floods in Northwestern Germany, and in early 2025, the catastrophic Los Angeles wildfires that were exacerbated by the record summer heat the year before followed by a severe drought.[8]

Scientists are growing more concerned about the potential shutdown of the Gulf Stream, which would have monumental global repercussions. Niklas Boers from the Potsdam Institute for Climate Impact Research in Germany, who conducted the research, stated, 'The signs of destabilisation being visible already is something that I wouldn't have expected and that I find alarming. It's something you just can't [allow to] happen.'[9] According to researchers, the complexity of the Gulf Stream and the uncertainty over future global heating levels make it impossible to predict an exact shutdown timeline. 'The currents are currently at their slowest point in at least 1,600 years, but the new analysis indicates they may be approaching a shutdown. This could occur within a decade or two, or several centuries from now.'[10]

While nobody can predict its timing, the consequences of such an event would be disastrous, severely disrupting global precipitation patterns essential for agriculture in India, South America and West Africa. Additionally, it would likely increase storm frequency and reduce temperatures in Europe, while raising sea levels along the eastern coast of North America.[11]

Not only are there already numerous deaths and victims due to extreme weather events; climate change is also a 'threat multiplier'. In the Sahel, climate change is having a devastating impact on the G5 countries (Mali, Chad, Niger, Mauritania and Burkina Faso), which are heavily dependent on rain-fed agriculture and pastoralism. By 2030, climate change will dry out the soil to the point where it can no longer absorb precipitation, reducing agricultural productivity.

A growing population of the G5 countries, which is expected to almost double by 2040, will increase pressure on these food systems and increase competition for resources. In the absence of strong governance structures and inclusive institutions, climate change can trigger distributional conflicts and violence. There will be no peace if the leaders of powerful countries are not attentive to the plight of the developing world and cooperate more in the fight against climate change.

THE IMPACT OF WAR

Russia's invasion of Ukraine led to the EU extending its reliance on fossil fuels. This situation underscores the importance of a strategy to mitigate such risks and prioritise environmental health. A Chatham House/OSCE paper examining the impact of the Ukraine War on climate security concluded that 'the war has also upended energy politics'.[12] Ukraine aimed to decrease its energy intensity[13] by two-thirds before the war. To improve energy efficiency will be even harder now that Russia has heavily damaged so much of its infrastructure. Rebuilding could help Ukraine leapfrog to a new energy infrastructure with efficient, low-carbon alternatives but it will take time. The war has caused increased greenhouse gas emissions.

The report highlighted potential spillover effects in other regions. A divide between authoritarian Russia/China and democratic NATO members could hinder efforts to manage Arctic climate changes. Global warming could lead to risks like the release of methane, a potent greenhouse gas, from melting permafrost.

Does anybody think a bigger war between two titans—China and the United States—and drawing in others would not set back efforts on climate change, perhaps for a generation or two? On the other hand, a global effort to fight climate change could reverse a slide into war by the US, Europe, China and Russia. The key is for leading nations to recognise their shared interest in planetary survival and act accordingly, using new technologies to benefit humanity instead of causing harm.

CHAPTER 8

Technology: The Best of Times?

A fundamental change has occurred in recent years: from embracing technological change several decades ago, the West is now a lot more fearful. Part of it came about because of globalisation. It wasn't just the 'China Shock' with its outsourcing of jobs. Automation did as much to kill jobs. Silicon Valley led the way with being super-optimistic that no matter the discovery or invention, it would all be good. That has changed. Scientists are split on how fast and far we should go with artificial intelligence that has the potential to limit or even erase humans. Killer robots are no longer science fiction. They could and are being designed to avoid casualties but inevitably people will be sidelined from decision-making by autonomous weapons.

There are also many opportunities. Ray Kurzweil, author of The Singularity is Near,[1] typified the early positive spirit. As he writes, 'By understanding the information processes underlying life, we are starting to learn to reprogramme our biology to achieve the virtual elimination of disease, the dramatic expansion of human potential and radical life extension.'

He defines 'singularity' as the convergence of several broad technologies—nano, bio, IT, AI, new materials and robotics—making this technology revolution different. The trigger was the computational advances that allowed such a wide array of different technologies to expand simultaneously, each feeding off the other. We should refer to the current situation as not one but many technology revolutions.

BIOTECHNOLOGY

We've had technology revolutions before, all have been disruptive in a positive and negative sense. This one has the potential to be transformational. Imagine paraplegics using their limbs thanks to an implanted microchip that picks up brain signals, decodes them and deploys a robotic arm or leg to regain movement. Similarly, with vision, there are several efforts using brain implants and computer interface technology. One involves connecting an implant to what looks like sunglasses.[2] The glasses process what the person would normally see and feed the information directly into the brain, restoring sight.

Robots will be particularly important for eldercare as working age populations decline in most advanced economies and some developing ones like China, Japan and South Korea. Those Asian countries are at the forefront of societal aging and are also investing heavily in robots. Finding ways to improve robots' sensory proficiencies and lower their cost will be important for improving quality of life.

Advances in biotech are important for finding cures that extend life. With the costs of sequencing genomes reduced, scientists can use big data to discover the genetic links to disease and help understand how to cure the sick. The cataloguing of individual genetic profiles will facilitate the development of new classes of targeted medicines.

Without the breakthroughs in gene sequencing, mRNA vaccines that were so effective against Covid-19 would not have been possible. A Chinese virologist Zhang Yongzhen shared the genomic sequence of SARS-CoV-2 with the world, accelerating vaccine development. Moreover, the manufacturing process for mRNA vaccines was much quicker. In the traditional process, a weakened version of the ailment, whether the Covid-19 virus or a disease like yellow fever, is injected into animal cells and grown in a laboratory. With this process, we would have needed millions of chicken eggs to develop the millions of doses of Covid vaccines. Even with modern fermentation equipment, it would have taken four to six weeks to manufacture a Covid vaccine. Manufacturing mRNA vaccines is a cell-free, biochemical process performed with synthetic enzymes that takes a matter of minutes. Many more people would have perished without the discovery of mRNA technology. Kurtzweil strongly believes that the human lifespan can be radically increased due to current and future breakthroughs in gene technology. Still, so far, the consensus among scientists is that there is an upper limit of around 122 years.[3]

CLIMATE TECH INNOVATIONS

While renewable energy is growing at exponential rates—415 per cent since 2000—it produces only 13 per cent of total world energy, which the IEA forecasts to grow to 20 per cent by 2030.[4] Fossil fuels—oil gas, coal—account for about 82 per cent of world energy production, are flat, not significantly declining.[5]

Some highly respected scientists don't think you can control climate change solely through emissions cuts and wholesale change out of fossils fuels into renewables. While 'emissions cuts are necessary', David Keith, a professor of applied physics and public policy at Harvard University, has written that 'pretending that climate change can be solved with emissions cuts alone is a dangerous fantasy. If you want to reduce risks from the emissions already in the atmosphere—whether that's to prevent forest fires in Algeria, heat waves in British Columbia or floods in Germany—you must look to carbon removal, solar geoengineering and local adaptation'.[6]

The problem with emissions is that they stay in the atmosphere for thousands of years. The draconian cuts in emissions only protect against any future warming. Today's cuts won't cool the world back down.

But here's where geopolitics intersects technological change. Other scientists than Keith worry that 'the current global governance system is unfit to develop and implement the far-reaching agreements needed to maintain fair, inclusive, and effective political control over solar geoengineering deployment'.[7] According to this rather sceptical view, UN multilateral bodies such as the General Assembly, the Environment Programme, and its Framework Convention on Climate Change cannot ensure fair and effective control over global solar geoengineering. The Security Council, dominated by five veto-wielding nations, lacks the legitimacy to regulate it effectively.

AI COMPETITION

The AI revolution has already created divisions and raised fears among some scientists. Nobel Prize winner Geoffrey Hinton is perhaps the best-known case of having been a pioneer of deep learning at Google. 'I have suddenly switched my views on whether these things are going to be more intelligent than us,' he writes, 'I think they're very close to it now and they will be much more intelligent than us in the future.' In conclusion, he asks, 'How do we survive that?'[8]

Hinton particularly fears that the machine learning tools he invented could be wrongfully used by malevolent forces. 'Look, here's one way it could all go wrong,' he says. 'We know that a lot of the people who want to use these tools are bad actors like Putin or [Florida Governor Ron] DeSantis. They want to use them for winning wars or manipulating electorates.' He adds, 'Don't think for a moment that Putin wouldn't make hyper-intelligent robots with the goal of killing Ukrainians, he wouldn't hesitate.'[9]

The late Henry Kissinger has also argued that AI could be 'far more devastating than even the biggest bomb, adding that there should be a 'new arms control process' to limit it.[10] He and the former head of Google Eric Schmidt warn that without constraints, AI will undo the Renaissance and the Enlightenment, taking human beings out of the decision making on how our societies run.

Already, any teacher knows that Chat GPT allows students to avoid researching or investigating for themselves, giving them an above average summary of the solutions to problems that students are meant to arrive at on their own. There are now calls for equal funding for AI safety to address AI's adverse effects and ensure balanced exploitation. This would curb the tech giants' rush to be first without safeguards against misuse. But it's unlikely that the warnings will be taken seriously until disaster happens. The internet was created without built-in security protection, resulting in extra costs for all of us trying to protect against scams. The US Federal Bureau of Investigation reported a record $12.5 billion in online scams in 2023-24.[11]

With technology, Americans tend to rush in, but the competition with China makes it virtually impossible that they will de-escalate despite the risks. The Biden administration tried to develop standards and a regulatory framework for 'safe and trustworthy AI' in issuing an executive order in 2023,[12] followed by a memorandum in 2024 to align AI with national security goals.[13] Biden put the National Institute for Standards and Technology at the centre of public-private partnership efforts to realise safe AI goals through a better understanding of ways to mitigate AI failures and evaluate safeguards such as developing a human-controlled off-switch.

Trump's governing approach isn't totally clear but during his campaign his team drafted a sweeping executive order that aims to boost military technology and reduce regulations on AI development. The draft order that the Washington Post obtained outlines a series of 'Manhattan Projects' to advance military AI capabilities. It calls for an immediate review of what it terms 'unnecessary and burdensome regulations' on AI development.[14]

Trump expressed concerns about AI becoming a 'superpower' and its potential dangers, including deepfakes, but acknowledged AI's inevitability and the need for America to compete with China. As mentioned, the Biden administration has also sought to limit China's technological progress in AI by restricting access to advanced chips. There is little doubt Trump will continue these efforts.

AI demands high computing power, requiring faster, smaller and more efficient transistors than standard central processing units. Advanced AI chips are essential for the efficient development and deployment of security-relevant AI systems. These chips enable rapid data processing from sensors, improving situational awareness and operational precision.[15]

Can America win the AI game against China using Western monopoly of state-of-the-art chipmaking? Early indications are that the US export controls on high-end chip have only invigorated Beijing's efforts to develop its own semiconductor capabilities. The US embargo on sales of high-end chipmaking devices and their chips are providing 'strong incentives for China—and to some extent for third parties that sell to China—to design out Western technology as much as the US is trying to deny Beijing access to its innovation'.[16] The chief executive of the American chips leader Nvidia Jensen Huang has already complained that his firm is losing future market share in China.[17] The chokepoint theory, which influences US policymakers from both Democratic and Republican parties, faces criticism. Outside of the policy sphere, many doubt that such chokepoints can persist for long. Semiconductor manufacturing primarily involves the application of science. 'There is more than one way of achieving one's goals; hence, there is no "secret sauce" that can protect anyone for long.[18] Restricting access to technology incentivises the replacement of it as shown by DeepSeek, a small Chinese artificial intelligence lab that designed a large language model on a bootstrapped budget.

The DeepSeek entrepreneur Liang Wenfeng wanted to prove that the Chinese can be creative, using only PhDs from top Chinese universities who had not gone to the United States. Ritwik Gupta, AI policy researcher at the University of California, Berkeley, said DeepSeek's recent model releases demonstrate that 'there is no moat when it comes to AI capabilities'.[19] 'The first person to train models has to expend lots of resources to get there,' he said. 'But the second mover can get there cheaper and more quickly.'[20] Gupta added that 'China had a much larger talent pool of systems engineers than the US who understand how to get the best use of computing resources to train and run models more cheaply.'[21]

Can Trump with his Manhattan Project control the development of AI? Already there are indications that the Pentagon has allowed AI-powered robots to get out of hand. What has happened with AI-powered robots cast doubt on controlling the technology. The Pentagon has said that it is committed to humans taking the final 'life or death decisions' in any AI-powered attack, but it looks as if we are rapidly sliding down a slippery slope. US defence officials are talking about 'oversight', not individual decisions as to whether to kill. According to a New York Times report, the Air Force secretary stated that drones and other arms will eventually need the capability to take lethal action autonomously, while remaining under human oversight. But he emphasised that 'Individual decisions versus not doing individual decisions is the difference between winning and losing—and you're not going to lose', pointing out that opponents would likely not impose such limitations on themselves, giving them a significant advantage.[22]

Such weapons must be operated in a defined geographic area for limited periods. If weapons are controlled by AI, military personnel should have the capability to deactivate systems that exhibit unintended behaviour. But humans are also capable of mistakes. Already operators, sometimes thousands of miles away, have made incorrect decisions, using missiles or drones to attack what they presumed were military targets mistaking, as often happened, a wedding party for a group of Taliban fighters in Afghanistan. But the software is being developed fast so that AI-guided drones can find and select targets on their own. Russia's jamming of radio communications and GPS in Ukraine is speeding up this advance, allowing drones to make its own decision without having to rely on communications from the attacking side.

US military leaders believe they must field 'autonomous systems in all domains—which are less expensive, put fewer people in the line of fire, and can be changed, updated, or improved with substantially shorter lead times' to compete with China's own investment in advanced weapons.[23]

Meanwhile, at the UN in New York and Geneva, there has been much talk but little action to enact legally binding rules on autonomous weapons. In December 2024, a record number of members voted in favour of the second UN General Assembly resolution on lethal autonomous weapons systems, but it will be an uphill battle to get a treaty with the major states leery of putting limits on their capabilities. Who's going to bet that such UN efforts will succeed in the face of increasing US-China competition?

DESTROYING JOBS

Technology waits for no one, and this goes for AI. Goldman Sachs in March 2023 forecasted that as many as 300 million full-time jobs around the world could be automated because of AI.[24] Administrative workers and lawyers are likely to be affected the most, not manual labourers in construction or agriculture. As happened in the 1990s with outsourcing, the effects will be more widespread in advanced economies, such as the US and Europe, where two-thirds of current jobs are exposed in some way to AI automation. The problem for businesses will again be finding AI-skilled workers and it's uncertain whether they will want to re-train existing workers.[25]

In the likely event of the removal of constraints on technology under Trump, he will aggravate the employment problem for his base which lacks the skills to thrive under AI.

Neither party has a solution for the education deficit. The results of the 2023 Trends in International Mathematics and Science Study (TIMSS) show that the US is falling behind leading countries like Japan, Singapore and Korea. Countries such as Poland, Sweden and Australia have overtaken America in some subjects. In math, American fourth graders' scores fell by 18 points and eighth graders' scores by 27 points, marking the largest decline since US participation in TIMSS began in 1995. The study also shows that the achievement gaps between the best and worst students in the US are widening.[26]

If the Democratic Party wants to regain its footing with the working and middle classes, here's an issue they can campaign on, equipping Americans for the unfolding AI revolution so that there are fewer losers. It's also a topic that local communities must focus on, upgrading community colleges so they attract today's students and equip them with skills that will allow them to weather the AI revolution.

EPILOGUE

Preparing for a New Age

There's no doubt we face perilous times, a historical inflection point: globalisation has broken into value-based trading networks; nationalism is growing everywhere, and major state-on-state war has returned while the shift from West to East along with a dizzying number of untested technologies is accelerating. With international cooperation declining, we have lost valuable time in combatting climate change endangering the planet and the quality of life for future generations. What are the hard lessons needed for changing the current self-interested directions of states towards cooperation?

LESSON #1:
AVOIDING WORLD WAR III

There are two ways the current impasse can be resolved: war, which the Harvard political scientist Graham Allison sees as the historic norm for settling differences between two rivals.[1] Under Biden, tensions flared and there were worries the United States and China were headed to a conflict over Taiwan, but both sides pulled back from the brink. Putin also raised the spectre of nuclear war with his repeated warnings of the use of tactical nuclear weapons to deter Western support for Ukraine.

The second way is to learn from the past two centuries of the great powers trying to live together in peace and apply them to international relations today. For the US, it must understand that global hegemony isn't tenable. The price for sustaining it would be bankruptcy at home and conflict abroad, possibly ending in a nuclear holocaust. The balance of power worked after the Concert of Europe: if followed today, the US would remain a great power but would have to recognise China and, over time, Russia as legitimate players, accepting too that the world is multipolar and America could not set all the rules.

Trump is far from giving up on the US right to order others around, but he favours fewer military interventions and is against 'forever wars', which is a step forward. He wants to bring peace to Ukraine and avoid any entanglement with China on Taiwan. In both cases it won't be easy. Even before becoming president, Trump has been working with the Israelis on a ceasefire for Gaza. Whether he can avoid a war with Iran will show his commitment to peace. To avoid future conflicts, arms control by the great powers will be imperative.

Sanctions should be gradually lifted on Russia and economic ties with the West reinstated once a solid peace is established between Moscow and a secure Kyiv. The US and West have too often delayed ending sanctions, adding new conditions for their abolition, and removing any incentives for those sanctioned. It will be difficult to let bygones be bygones but Europe must not seek to 'cancel' out Russia by keeping barriers up which would make a permanent peace impossible and drive Russia more into the arms of China.

A US China expert suggested Washington should state it approves of Taiwan's unification with China if achieved peacefully. This would counter China's belief that military force is the only way to avoid Taiwanese independence. Yet in recent years, Washington has gone from helping Taiwan defend itself to claiming the island as a strategic asset which it cannot lose without undermining its naval superiority in East Asia. As mentioned earlier, it may take a Cuban Missile Crisis-like event to persuade both sides to dial back the ruinous security competition and inaugurate confidence-building measures.

The Middle East is perhaps the hardest of the three conflicts given the number of players and long-running wars. Annexation of Palestinian territories will only foment additional unrest. Five million Palestinians cannot be suppressed forever. Hamas and Hezbollah aren't likely to disappear, even if they have been severely weakened. Indeed, in the waning days of the Biden administration, Secretary of State Blinken said the US government assessed that 'Hamas has recruited almost as many new fighters as it has lost'.[2] Palestinian self-rule on the West Bank and Gaza is the only solution. Israel should take the help offered by Saudi Arabia, the US and others to establish a Palestinian state that is strong enough to stop terrorists from operating from its territory. It may take some time for Israelis to tire of an unrelenting conflict. Yet taking steps to annex the West Bank and Gaza could ignite strife between Palestinians and Jews inside Israel. The Trump administration won't want to pressure Israel, but Europeans, Saudis and others should step in and convince the Trump administration against any recognition of annexation by the Israelis.

The United States has sought too often to implement regime change with its enemies. Cornering Iran will only fast-track its resolve to produce nuclear weapons. Washington would do better to reach out, as Trump has mentioned in the campaign, but it will need to avoid the maximum pressure tactics which, instead of softening up Tehran, will result in another failed attempt at cooperation. Russia and China play increasing roles and would need to be engaged in an effort at regional peace.

LESSON #2:
COOPERATION OVER COMPETITION

Climate mitigation and adaptation efforts offer another chance to renew US-China relations and build trust. Protecting oneself while ignoring global climate struggles is unsustainable. This must be a worldwide effort; success depends on it. China's role in green technology makes its cooperation vital. Why shouldn't the US and Europeans explore joint efforts with the Chinese and others, for example, for the development of better and more long-lasting batteries? Without better batteries, the transition to green technologies will stall. To succeed with the energy transition, scientists estimate the need for 'a couple of hundred terawatt-hours, which is at least a hundred times more capacity than we have today'.[3] Most batteries today rely on lithium and cobalt, the latter mined sometimes in awful conditions, such as in Congo where child labour is used. There is already widespread research but why not accelerate efforts through enhanced international scientific cooperation commissioned by a consortium of the major powers or the entire G-20?

Yet the United States fears an expansion of China's near monopoly on battery production and wants to wean Western countries off any reliance on China and produce its own. Rather than competing with one another, some key technological innovations should be shared as public goods for everyone's benefit.

American, Asian and European green technology value

chains could be severely impacted if the US-China trade war escalates. True leadership in our multipolar world involves addressing global issues, not just self-interest. The West must show it considers broader interests beyond its own to maintain influence. Isolating behind its own 'democracy wall' and ignoring the wider world will hinder the spread of Western values and undermine our economic foundations.

China has become the global renewable energy leader within the past decade and is expected to exceed its 2030 solar and wind energy target already in 2025.[4] Its more affordable renewables are pivotal for the clean energy transition in the developing world. But coal plants are also increasing, partly as backup for all the new wind and solar farms, along with China being the biggest emitter of greenhouse gases. Despite its progress, China too must do more. Russia has the most potential for solar, wind and nuclear energies, but government's reliance on oil and gas revenues to fund the Ukraine war is a big obstacle to the green energy transition. Instead of confrontation, more cooperation is needed to tackle global climate change and prevent another financial crisis.

LESSON #3:
AVOIDING THE NEXT FINANCIAL CRISIS

The US and the West took a tumble when the 2007-08 financial crisis hit. China's economic weight was a godsend then to help the West and global economy get out of its rut. China inflated, pulling others up. For Beijing, the financial crisis was proof of Western and America's decline.

In today's multipolar world international coordination would again be needed to reduce worsening macroeconomic imbalances, which have the potential to turn into a crisis. These risks were evident during the global economic and financial crisis of 2007-08, when global imbalances were large[5] and a key factor in the spread of the crisis. Then US Treasury Secretary Hank Paulson Jr. said, 'If we only address particular regulatory issues—as critical as they are—without addressing the global imbalances that fuelled recent excesses, we will have missed an opportunity to dramatically improve the foundation for global markets and economic vitality going forward. The pressure from global imbalances will simply build up again until it finds another outlet'.[6]

Imbalances are on the rise and won't be reduced by Trump's tariffs and decoupling supply chains, but by long-term, structural adjustment processes: surplus countries such as Germany and China should save less and consume more. Such a move by Germany would also strengthen Europe's political unity. Chinese leaders are only likely to favour a turn towards a consumer-led economy if tensions with the US ease. Deficit countries such as the US should save more and reduce government deficits and debt which are also promoting macroeconomic imbalances.

As long as the US has a budget deficit it will have trade deficits, and the twin deficits—budget and trade—are in part a consequence of strong dollar. Hence measures should be taken to reduce the structural overvaluation of the dollar as well as force a correction of the undervalued Chinese yuan. John Maynard Keynes proposed a global trade and capital regime in 1944 that involved a synthetic currency designed to absorb global imbalances, such a supranational currency based on the Special Drawing Rights of the International Monetary Fund. Yet none of the major players—the US, the EU and China—will want to coordinate their monetary and fiscal policies in such an arrangement which would be seen by all of them as a loss of sovereignty.

Even another Plaza Accord that sought to appreciate yuan

against the dollar and try to cut back on Chinese exports is unlikely. The 1985 Plaza Accord was a deal struck by Washington with its allies to bail out the US by appreciating their own currencies. America was in a similar situation as today, roiled by the inflation and suffering high fiscal and trade deficits. China has no doubt absorbed the lesson that Japan learned. In helping out the US, Japan increased the value of the yen, making its exports unaffordable and ushering in the long deflationary decade at home.

More practicable may be an informal but regularised trilateral mechanism by the Big Three—United States, European Union and China—central bank and treasury heads for sharing views views on the threats to global financial stability and needed macroeconomic changes that each should take. Establishing such routine high-level confidential exchanges won't necessarily prevent another financial crisis but could help accelerate the rapid decision making needed if a crisis unfolds. As in 2008, financial crises often require quick agreements to avoid further escalation. The routinised three-way high-level discussions would also build trust and facilitate solutions to other problems such as the debt crisis in poorer countries.

LESSON #4:
INCLUSIVITY: A MORE REPRESENTATIVE MULTILATERAL SYSTEM

Historically, the best time for multilateral reform was when there is a recognised global hegemon. Paradoxically with multipolarity, it is harder to reform with various rising powers vying for a permanent seat and suspicious of changes that could favour their opponents. Therefore, the reform of the UN Security Council has been stymied. While UN membership has risen from 51 to 185 countries, Security Council seats have only increased from

11 to 15 in the mid-1960s. The five permanent members were victors in the Second World War and each retains a veto. The 10 non-permanent members represent different regions and only serve for two years.

There may be a route out of this which could unlock changes favouring more Global South representation. The African Union and G4 representing Brazil, Germany, India and Japan should agree on a common approach, including showing flexibility on their demand for a veto, then the P5 would face pressure to come to a decision. China and Russia—both of which claim to support Global South interests—would lose credibility if they opposed a combined AU/G4 while Western P3 have an opportunity to take the initiative, thawing ties between them and the Global South over Ukraine. The P3 would show that they recognise the injustice of current leadership makeup of many of the Western-founded multilaterals.

Without such reform of the UNSC and other multilateral institutions developing countries would tend to put more hope and trust in Russian and Chinese founded bodies such as the BRICS where their voices are more likely to be heard. Competing multilateral bodies will increase confrontation and undermine cooperation necessary to enable a sustainable and peaceful future.

Woodrow Wilson, the 28th President of United States, failed to achieve a new, more peaceful world order at the end of World War I, not least because of the domestic restrictions against the US joining the League of Nations and assuming a bigger global role. Isolationist and protectionist voices prevailed in US foreign policy—one that was unilateral and inward-looking, disentangling itself from 'extra-hemispheric' security commitments and turning away from international economic cooperation. We all know how this story ended: a second world war.

If we fail to act decisively, history will not simply repeat—it will accelerate, pulling us into an era of unprecedented conflict, economic instability, and environmental devastation. The lessons of the past demand more from us. Cooperation is no longer just an option; it is an imperative.

It is not just about avoiding catastrophe; it is about forging a future where shared prosperity, security, and sustainability become the foundation of a truly global order. The alternative is not merely failure—it is the collapse of everything we value.

Endnotes

PREFACE

1. Aaron Zitner and Xavier Martinez, Voters Want MAGA Lite From Trump, WSJ Poll Finds, Wall Street Journal, 17 January 2025, https://www.wsj.com/politics/policy/donald-trump-policy-approval-poll-849feb84?page=1.

2. Donald Trump, Second Inaugural Speech, Annotated, New York Times, 20 January 2025, https://www.nytimes.com/interactive/2025/01/20/us/trump-inauguration-speech-annotated.html.

3. Branko Milanović, How the Mainstream Abandoned Universal Economic Principles (But Forgot to Mention It), Global Inequality and More 3.0 Blog, 8 January 2025, https://branko2f7.substack.com/p/how-the-mainstream-has-abandoned?utm_source=post-email-title&publication_id=371309&post_id=154385191&utm_campaign=email-post-title&isFreemail=true&r=1u308u&triedRedirect=true&utm_medium=email.

INTRODUCTION

1. Seventy Years of U.S. Public Opinion on the United Nations, Roper Centre for Public Opinion Research, 22 June 2015, https://ropercentre.cornell.edu/blog/seventy-years-us-public-opinion-united-nations. Also see Albert Trethart and Olivia Case, Do People Trust the UN? A Look at the Data, 22 February 2023, https://theglobalobservatory.org/2023/02/do-people-trust-the-un-a-look-at-the-data/.

2. Op. cit. Donald Trump, Second Inaugural Speech.

3. Barak Ravid and David Lawler, Scoop: Denmark Sent Trump Team Private Messages on Greenland, Axios, 11 January 2025, https://www.axios.com/2025/01/11/denmark-response-trump-greenland-threat.

4. See Stephen Wertheim, WWIII Begins With Forgetting, New York Times, 2 December 2022, https://www.nytimes.com/2022/12/02/opinion/america-world-war-iii.html. Around 1 percent of US veterans of World War II remain and unlike that war generation, most Americans know only Iraq and Afghanistan wars, not the specter of a nuclear confrontation that earlier President Kennedy and Truman faced and sought to avert.

5. United Nations Environmental Programmeme, Emissions Gap Report 2023, 20 November 2023, https://www.unep.org/resources/emissions-gap-report-2023.

6. James Carville, I Was Wrong About the 2024 Election. Here's Why, New York Times, 2 January 2025, https://www.nytimes.com/2025/01/02/opinion/democrats-donald-trump-economy.html?searchResultPosition=1.

CHAPTER 1: THE END OF A DREAM

1. Juliana Menasce Horowitz, Ruth Igielnik and Rakesh Kochhar, Trends in Income and Wealth Inequality, Pew Research Centre, 9 January 2020, https://www.pewresearch.org/social-trends/2020/01/09/trends-in-income-and-wealth-inequality/.

2. Peter Arcidiacono, Josh Kinsler and Tyler Ransom, Legacy and Athlete Preferences at Harvard, National Bureau of Economic Research (NBER) Working Paper Series, No 26316, Cambridge, MA September 2019, https://www.nber.org/system/files/working_papers/w26316/w26316.pdf.

3. The Opportunity Atlas, an interactive tool, developed by the U.S. Census Bureau (https://www.census.gov/library/stories/2018/10/opportunity-atlas.html) in collaboration with researchers from Harvard and Brown University, provides highly localized data on social mobility. It shows that moving early in life to a neighbourhood with better overall outcomes can increase a child's income by several thousand dollars later in life.

4. Ayesha Rascoe, The Racial Income Gap Has Narrowed for Black Americans, New Research Shows, NPR, 4 August 2024, https://www.npr.org/2024/08/04/nx-s1-5059187/the-racial-income-gap-has-narrowed-for-black-americans-new-research-shows.

5. Scott Lincicome, Grading Trump's Economic Policies, Cato Commentary, Cato Institute, 16 October 2020, https://www.cato.org/commentary/grading-trumps-economic-policies#.

6. Committee for a Responsible Federal Budget, Analysis of CBO's March 2024 Long-Term Budget Outlook, 20 March 2024, https://www.crfb.org/papers/analysis-cbos-march-2024-long-term-budget-outlook.

7. Congressional Budget Office (CBO), Climate Change, https://www.cbo.gov/topics/climate-and-environment/climate-change.

8. Candace Vahlsing and Zach Liscow, The Importance of Measuring the Fiscal and Economic Costs of Climate Change, The White House, Office of

Management and Budget (OMB), 14 March 2023, https://www.whitehouse.gov/omb/briefing-room/2023/03/14/the-importance-of-measuring-the-fiscal-and-economic-costs-of-climate-change/.

9. By Laura H. Gillam and Wesley E. Yin, Responding to the Financial Impacts of Climate Change, The White House, Office of Management and Budget (OMB), 22 April 2024, https://www.whitehouse.gov/omb/briefing-room/2024/04/22/responding-to-the-financial-impacts-of-climate-change/.

10. Farid Guliyev, Trump's 'America First' Energy Policy, Contingency and the Reconfiguration of the Global Energy Order, Energy Policy, Vol. 140, May 2020, https://doi.org/10.1016/j.enpol.2020.11143.

11. Nicole Narea, Biden Isn't Advertising America's Record Oil Boom, Vox, 13 March 2024, https://www.vox.com/climate/24098983/biden-oil-production-climate-fossil-fuel-renewables.

12. Catherine Rampell, A 'War on American Energy'? So Why Is Oil Production Near Record Highs?, Washington Post, 3 October 2023, https://www.washingtonpost.com/opinions/2023/10/03/biden-fossil-fuels-republicans-energy-war-record/.

13. Lisa Friedman, Biden Bans New Oil and Gas Drilling Along Most U.S. Coasts, New York Times, 6 January 2025, https://www.nytimes.com/2025/01/06/climate/biden-oil-gas-drilling-ban.html?searchResultPosition=2.

14. Princeton University studies have found that recent US tariffs have been passed on entirely to US importers and consumers, leading to higher prices: Mary Amiti, Stephen J. Redding and David E. Weinstein, Who's Paying for the US Tariffs? A Longer-Term Perspective, AEA Papers and Proceedings 2020, 110: pp. 541–546, https://doi.org/10.1257/pandp.20201018; A PIIE analysis highlights that Trump's tariffs, including a proposed universal baseline tariff, would increase costs for US consumers and businesses: Warwick J. McKibbin, Megan Hogan and Marcus Noland, The international economic implications of a second Trump presidency, Peterson Institute for International Economics (PIIE) Working Papers 24-20, September 2024, https://www.piie.com/publications/working-papers/2024/international-economic-implications-second-trump-presidency.

15. According to FactCheck.org, a project of the Annenberg Public Policy Centre, the international trade deficit for goods and services went up 22.3 percent under Biden; Brooks Jackson, Eugene Kiely, D'Angelo Gore, Lori Robertson and Robert Farley, Biden's Numbers, July 2024 Update, 25 July 2024, https://www.factcheck.org/2024/07/bidens-numbers-july-2024-update/.

16. Op. cit. Donald Trump, Second Inaugural Speech.

17. Agenda47: Preventing World War III, 16 March 2023, https://www.donaldjtrump.com/agenda47/agenda47-preventing-world-war-iii.

18. Branko Milanović, The ideology of Donald J. Trump, Global Inequality

and More 3.0 Blog, 12 November 2024, https://branko2f7.substack.com/p/the-ideology-of-donald-j-trump?utm_source=substack&publication_id=371309&post_id=151536896&utm_medium=email&utm_content=share&utm_campaign=email-share&triggerShare=true&isFreemail=true&r=1u308u&triedRedirect=true.

19. The phrase was coined by Secretary of State Madeleine Albright. It has mostly been a shibboleth of conservative politicians up until recently when the belief is more deeply held by the Democratic establishment than MAGA Republicans.

20. Op. cit. Donald Trump, Second Inaugural Speech.

21. Ibid.

22. The Biden-Trump election impact on K-12 education highlighted that both administrations faced challenges in addressing the homework gap and connecting all students to the internet. It became clear that more permanent solutions were needed to close the gap and address the educational losses from the pandemic: Matt Zalaznick, How will the 2020 Biden-Trump election impact K-12?, District Administration, 20 October 2020, https://districtadministration.com/article/how-will-the-2020-biden-trump-election-impact-k-12/. Despite Biden's historic investments in public education through the American Rescue Plan, there are still significant challenges in addressing the educational losses from the pandemic. The plan set aside nearly $170 billion for public schools, but the effectiveness of these funds in making up for the losses in basic English and mathematics remains a concern. Amanda Litvinov, Three Years In, Biden's American Rescue Plan Buoys Millions of Students and Educators, NEA Today, 11 March 2024, https://www.nea.org/nea-today/all-news-articles/three-years-bidens-american-rescue-plan-buoys-millions-students-and-educators.

23. Patrick J. Lyons, Isabelle Taft and Eileen Sullivan, Trump Plans to Put an End to Birthright Citizenship. That Could Be Hard, New York Times, 20 January 2025, https://www.nytimes.com/2025/01/20/us/politics/can-trump-end-birthright-citizenship-not-easily.html?searchResultPosition=2.

24. RealFacts Editorial Team, Industries at Risk: The Economic Fallout of Trump Intended Immigration Crackdowns, 26 November 2024, https://www.realfacts.com/post/industries-at-risk-the-economic-fallout-of-trump-intended-immigration-crackdowns; Alexina Cather, How Trump's Promises of Mass Deportations Could Impact the Food System, Hunter College New York City Policy Centre, 13 November 2024, https://www.nycfoodpolicy.org/how-trumps-promises-of-mass-deportations-could-impact-the-food-system/.

25. Edward Segal, How A Mass Deportation Of Immigrants Would Impact Businesses, Forbes, 18 November 2024, https://www.forbes.com/sites/edwardsegal/2024/11/17/how-a-mass-deportation-of-immigrants-could-impact-businesses/.

26. Jackie DeFusco, Trump Backs Foreign Worker Visa Programme Splitting His Supporters, WDSU, 29 December 2024, https://www.wdsu.com/article/trump-h1b-visa-debate/63299446.

27. Op. cit. Donald Trump, Second Inaugural Speech.

28. Ibid.

29. Asawin Suebsaeng and Andrew Perez, Team Trump Debates How Much Should We Invade Mexico, Rolling Stone, 27 November 2024, https://www.rollingstone.com/politics/politics-features/trump-mexico-drug-cartels-military-invade-1235183177/.

30. Op. cit., Aaron Zitner and Xavier Martinez, Voters Want MAGA Lite From Trump.

31. Michael Sainato, 'They would not listen to us': Inside Arizona's Troubled Chip Plant, The Guardian, 28 August 2023, https://www.theguardian.com/business/2023/aug/28/phoenix-microchip-plant-biden-union-tsmc.

32. Brian Kennedy and Alec Tyson, How Republicans View Climate Change and Energy Issues, Pew Research Centre, 1 March 2024, https://www.pewresearch.org/short-reads/2024/03/01/how-republicans-view-climate-change-and-energy-issues/.

33. Op. cit. Donald Trump, Second Inaugural Speech.

34. Colin Grabow, Inflation Another Reason to Rethink Buy American Protectionism, Cato at Liberty Blog, 20 April 2022, https://www.cato.org/blog/touting-buy-american-protectionism-inflation-antidote-economic-quackery.

35. Gary Clyde Hufbauer, Megan Hogan and Yilin Wang, For Inflation Relief, the United States Should Look to Trade Liberalization, Peterson Institute for International Economics (PIIE) Policy Brief, March 2022, https://www.piie.com/sites/default/files/documents/pb22-4.pdf.

36. Joshua Chaffin and Deborah Acosta, How a Real Estate Mogul Became Trump's Middle East Point Man, Wall Street Journal, 17 November 2024, https://www.wsj.com/politics/elections/trump-transition-witkoff-middle-east-39364c30?mod=hp_lead_pos8.

37. Molly Nagle and Kelsey Walsh, Administration Official Shares Inside Story of How Hamas-Israel Deal Came About, ABCNews, 15 January 2025, https://abcnews.go.com/Politics/white-house-official-shares-inside-story-hamas-israel/story?id=117723507.

38. While Iran's President Masoud Pezeshkian said Tehran will not be able to ignore its arch-foe, the United States, and needs to 'handle its enemies with forbearance,' Trump had said during his election campaign, 'I don't want to do damage to Iran but they cannot have nuclear weapons.' Iran's President Says Tehran Has to Deal With Washington, Reuters / US News, 12 November

2024, https://www.usnews.com/news/world/articles/2024-11-12/iran-says-it-will-pursue-its-interest-when-asked-about-possibility-of-trump-talks. Yet Trump cautioned against U.S. efforts at regime change in Tehran and just days after the U.S. presidential election, Elon Musk, a close confidant of the president-elect, met with Iran's ambassador to the United Nations to discuss reducing tensions between Tehran and Washington. Jon Hoffman, Time Is Running Out For Iran-US Diplomacy. Trump Should Strike a Deal With Iran, The Hill, 30 December 2024, https://thehill.com/opinion/5059043-trump-diplomacy-iran-nuclear/.

39. Ksenia Svetlova, How Iraq Became the Top Link in China's Belt and Road Strategy, The Media Line, 6 February 2022, https://themedialine.org/top-stories/how-iraq-became-the-top-link-in-beijings-belt-and-road-strategy/.

40. Ibid.

41. Didi Tang, Trump Says Taiwan Should Pay More For Defence and Dodges Questions If He Would Defend the Island, Associated Press, 18 July 2024, https://apnews.com/article/trump-taiwan-chips-invasion-china-910e7a94b19248fc75e5d1ab6b0a34d8.

42. Didi Tang, China's Xi Is Likely To Decline Trump's Inauguration Invitation, Seeing It As Too Risky To Attend, The Hill, 24 December 2024, https://thehill.com/homenews/ap/ap-international/ap-chinas-xi-is-likely-to-decline-trumps-inauguration-invitation-seeing-it-as-too-risky-to-attend/

CHAPTER 2: RUSSIA AND EUROPE UNDER TRUMP

1. Four empires include Kievan Rus' that stretched from the White Sea in the North to the Black Sea in the South and from the headwaters of the Vistula in the West to the Taman Peninsula in the East, uniting the East Slavic tribes. The Mongol invasion of Kievan Rus in 1237–1240 inaugurated the rule of The Khan of the Golden Horde until 1480 when Ivan III freed Russia from the Mongols and later Ivan the Terrible expanded Muscovite territory into Siberia. After him there was a time of troubles before the establishment in 1613 of the Romanov dynasty. In 1721, Peter the Great was named Emperor of all Russia. From then on, the Russian empire had a Tsar or Tsarina who ruled as an absolute monarch. By the end of the 1800s, the Russian Empire covered almost 1/6 of all the land on earth. The Russian Empire ended in 1917 with the Revolution. The Union of Soviet Socialist Republics or U.S.S.R. was a union of fifteen national republics with a highly centralized Communist government based in Moscow. The U.S.S.R. fell apart in 1991 and became the Russian Federation. Many republics, such as Estonia, Latvia, Ukraine, and others, became independent, but the Russian Federation remains the largest country by far in landmass stretching across two continents with the ninth largest population in the world. It has 21 internationally recognised ethnic republics plus the Republic of Crimea. See Philip Longworth, Russia's Empires: Their Rise and Fall From Prehistory to Putin, London: John Murray, 2006.

2. A public opinion survey conducted by the Chicago Council on Global Affairs and the Levada Analytical Centre in September 2024 found that a plurality of Russians now think the conflict in Ukraine has more disadvantages than advantages for their country. A slight majority (54 percent) support the Kremlin moving to peace negotiations, but the results suggest that everyday Russians want a peace agreement to cement Russia's battlefield gains—not to make any meaningful concessions to Kyiv. Dina Smeltz, Lama El Baz and Denis Volkov, Russians More Interested in Peace Talks with Ukraine, but Most Oppose Making Major Concessions, Chicago Council on Global Affairs, 9 October 2024, https://globalaffairs.org/research/public-opinion-survey/russians-more-interested-peace-talks-ukraine-most-oppose-making.

3. Samuel Charap and Sergey Radchenko, The Talks That Could Have Ended the War in Ukraine. A Hidden History of Diplomacy That Came Up Short—But Holds Lessons For Future Negotiations, in Foreign Affairs, 16 April 2024, https://www.foreignaffairs.com/ukraine/talks-could-have-ended-war-ukraine.

4. Mathew Burrows, European Security Post-Ukraine War, Stimson Policy Memo, 9 August 2024, https://www.stimson.org/2024/european-security-post-ukraine-war/.

5. Quoted in: Op. cit. Samuel Charap and Sergey Radchenko, The Talks That Could Have Ended the War in Ukraine.

6. Virginia Page Fortna, Does Peacekeeping Work? Shaping Belligerents' Choices after Civil War, Princeton University Press, 2008.

7. Irina Slav, China and India Account for More Than 90% of Russian Oil and Fuel Exports, 27 December 2023, Oilprice.com, https://oilprice.com/Latest-Energy-News/World-News/China-and-India-Account-for-More-Than-90-of-Russian-Oil-and-Fuel-Exports.html.

8. Timothy Helenjak, Eeva Turunen and Shinan Wang, Cities on Ice: Population Change in Arctic, Nordregio Magazine, https://nordregio.org/nordregio-magazine/issues/arctic-changes-and-challenges/cities-on-ice-population-change-in-the-arctic/.

9. U.S. Energy Information Administration (EIA), Arctic Oil and Natural Gas Resources, 20 January 2012, https://www.eia.gov/todayinenergy/detail.php?id=4650.

10. Nathan Hodge, The CIA Chief Says Putin Is 'Entirely Too Healthy.' What Do We Really Know About His Condition? CNN, 21 July 2022, https://www.cnn.com/2022/07/21/europe/vladimir-putin-health-cia-cmd-intl/index.html.

11. Curtis Williams, US Was Top LNG Exporter in 2023 As Hit Record Levels, in: Reuters, 3 January 2024, https://www.reuters.com/business/energy/us-was-top-lng-exporter-2023-hit-record-levels-2024-01-02/.

12. White House, Fact Sheet Biden-Harris Administration Announces Temporary Pause on Pending Approvals of Liquefied Natural Gas

Exports, Washington, DC, 26 January 2024, https://www.whitehouse.gov/briefing-room/statements-releases/2024/01/26/fact-sheet-biden-harris-administration-announces-temporary-pause-on-pending-approvals-of-liquefied-natural-gas-exports/.

13. Timothy Gardner, Biden Pauses LNG Export Approvals After Pressure From Climate Activists, in: Reuters, 26 January 2024, https://www.reuters.com/business/energy/biden-pauses-approval-new-lng-export-projects-win-climate-activists-2024-01-26/.

14. Jennifer Jacobs and Peter Martin, Trump Eyes NATO Makeover, Hurried Peace in Ukraine If Elected, in: Bloomberg, 14 February 2024, https://www.bloomberg.com/news/articles/2024-02-14/trump-eyes-two-tier-nato-security-pledge-zelenskiy-putin-peace-talks-if-elected.

15. Isaac Arnsdorf, Josh Dawsey and Michael Birnbaum, Inside Donald Trump's Secret, Long-shot Plan to End the War in Ukraine, in: Washington Post, 7 April 2024, https://www.washingtonpost.com/politics/2024/04/05/trump-ukraine-secret-plan/.

16. Jamie McIntyre, Vance Says Trump's Plan to End the War Would Likely Force Ukraine To Give Up Land, NATO aspirations in: Washington Examiner, 13 September 2024, https://www.msn.com/en-us/news/world/vance-says-trump-s-plan-to-end-the-war-would-likely-force-ukraine-to-give-up-land-nato-aspirations/ar-AA1qvNSS.

17. Clayton Vickers, Trump Defends NATO Threats As 'a Form of Negotiation', in: The Hill, 19 March 2024, https://thehill.com/policy/international/4542440-trump-defends-nato-threats-as-a-form-of-negotiation/.

18. The United States' national debt almost doubled in the last decade from just under $18 trillion in 2014, and since doubled again to over $36 trillion today. U.S. Department of the Treasury, Fiscal Data, https://fiscaldata.treasury.gov/americas-finance-guide/national-debt/.

19. Xi Sets Targets for China's Science, Technology Progress, China Daily, 30 May 2016, https://www.chinadaily.com.cn/china/2016-05/30/content_25540484.htm; Laura Zhou and Orange Wang, How 'Made in China 2025' Became a Lightning Rod in 'War Over China's National Destiny', South China Morning Post, 18 January 2019, https://www.scmp.com/news/china/diplomacy/article/2182441/how-made-china-2025-became-lightning-rod-war-over-chinas.

CHAPTER 3: FROM CHIMERICA TO CHINA SHOCK

1. Niall Ferguson and Moritz Schularick, The End of Chimerica, Harvard Business School Working Paper, No. 10-037, November 2009.

2. Helmut Reisen, Shifting Wealth: Is the U.S. Dollar Empire Falling?, VoxEu.org, 20 June 2009, https://cepr.org/voxeu/columns/shifting-wealth-us-dollar-empire-falling.

3. Maurice Obstfeld, Jay Shambaugh and Alan Taylor, Financial Instability, Reserves, and Central Bank Swap Lines in the Panic of 2008, Paper Presented at the ASSA Meetings, January 2009, American Economic Review, Papers and Proceedings, p. 30; Michael Pettis, China's Great Demand Challenge, Far Eastern Economic Review, January 2009, pp. 8-13.

4. Greenspan Admits 'Mistake' That Helped Crisis, NBC News, 23 October 2008, https://www.nbcnews.com/id/wbna27335454.

5. David H. Autor, David Dorn and Gordon H. Hanson, The China Shock: Learning from Labor Market Adjustment to Large Changes in Trade, National Bureau of Economic Research Working Paper, January 2016, https://www.nber.org/papers/w21906.

6. Ibid.

7. Adam S. Posen, The Price of Nostalgia. America's Self-Defeating Economic Retreat, Foreign Affairs, May/June 2021, Published on 20 April 2021; https://www.foreignaffairs.com/articles/united-states/2021-04-20/america-price-nostalgia.

8. Ibid.

9. Richard Baldwin, China Is the World's Sole Manufacturing Superpower: A Line Sketch of the Rise, CEPR, 17 January 2024, https://cepr.org/voxeu/columns/china-worlds-sole-manufacturing-superpower-line-sketch-rise.

10. Peter Dizikes, Q&A: David Autor On the Long Afterlife of the 'China Shock,' MIT News, 6 December 2021, https://news.mit.edu/2021/david-autor-china-shock-persists-1206.

11. Iman Ghosh, How China Overtook the US and the World's Major Trading Partner, Visual Capitalist, 22 January 2020, https://www.visualcapitalist.com/china-u-s-worlds-trading-partner/#:~:text=How%20China%20Overtook%20the%20U.S.%20as%20the%20World%E2%80%99s%20Major%20Trading%20Partner.

12. Ibid.

13. James McBride and Andrew Chatzky, Is 'Made in China 2025' a Threat to Global Trade?, Council on Foreign Relations (CFR) Backgrounder, 13 May 2019, https://www.cfr.org/backgrounder/made-china-2025-threat-global-trade.

14. Francois de Soyres and Dylan Moore, Assessing China's Efforts to Increase Self-Reliance, FEDS Notes, Federal Reserve of the United States, 2 February 2024, https://www.federalreserve.gov/econres/notes/feds-notes/assessing-chinas-efforts-to-increase-self-reliance-20240202.html.

15. Carol Ryan, OPEC Cartel Has Nothing on China's Clean-Energy Monopoly, Wall Street Journal, 16 January 2023, https://www.wsj.com/articles/opec-cartel-has-nothing-on-chinas-clean-energy-monopoly-11673883488.

16. Agnes Chang and Keith Bradsher, Can the World Make an Electric Car Battery Without China? New York Times, 16 May 2023, https://www.nytimes.com/interactive/2023/05/16/business/china-ev-battery.html?searchResultPosition=2.

17. Víctor Burguete, China and the Global South: Trade, Investment and Rescue Loans, Barcelona Centre for International Affairs, November 2023, https://www.cidob.org/en/publications/china-and-global-south-trade-investment-and-rescue-loans.

18. Belt and Road Economics: Opportunities and Risks of Transport Corridors, World Bank, 18 June 2019, https://www.worldbank.org/en/topic/regional-integration/publication/belt-and-road-economics-opportunities-and-risks-of-transport-corridors.

19. World Bank Group Releases FY22 Audited Financial Statements, 8 August 2022, https://www.worldbank.org/en/news/press-release/2022/08/08/world-bank-group-releases-fy22-audited-financial-statements#:~:text=IBRD's loan portfolio increased to $227.1 billion%2C, well above the prudential minimum liquidity level.

20. International Infrastructure Projects: China's Investments Significantly Outpace the U.S., and Experts Suggest Potential Improvements to the U.S. Approach, U.S. Government Accountability Office, 12 September 2024, https://www.gao.gov/products/gao-24-106866#:~:text=What GAO Found. From 2013 to 2021%2C,provided $76 billion in the same sectors.

21. Jonathan D. Moyer, Collin J. Meisel, Austin S. Matthews, David K. Bohl, and Mathew J. Burrows, China-US Competition: Measuring Global Influence, Atlantic Council, Washington, DC, May 2021, https://www.atlanticcouncil.org/wp-content/uploads/2021/06/China-US-Competition-Report-2021.pdf.

22. Ibid.

23. Jason Douglas, China Has Limited Firepower to Counter U.S. Tariffs, Wall Street Journal, 29 December 2024, https://www.wsj.com/economy/trade/china-has-limited-firepower-to-counter-u-s-tariffs-108df7e9?page=1.

24. Ma Jihua, a veteran industry analyst and a close follower of China's chip industry, told the Global Times: GT Yearender: China Stands Firm Against Relentless US Crackdown in 2022, Global Times, 29 December 2022, https://www.globaltimes.cn/page/202212/1282912.shtml.

25. Christopher Johnson, Why China Will Play It Safe, Foreign Affairs, 14 November 2022, https://www.foreignaffairs.com/china/why-china-will-play-it-safe.

26. Edward Luce, Containing China Is Biden's Explicit Goal, Financial Times, 19 October 2022, https://www.ft.com/content/398f0d4e-906e-479b-a9a7-e4023c298f39.

27. Irvine H. Anderson, Jr., The 1941 De Facto Embargo on Oil to Japan:

A Bureaucratic Reflex, Pacific Historical Review (1975) 44 (2): pp. 201–231, https://doi.org/10.2307/3638003.

28. Jacqueline Deal, Trump, Congress Must Fix the National Emergency that Biden Declared, The Hill, 9 December 2024, https://thehill.com/opinion/5029506-biden-executive-order-china-technology/; Robert Higgs, How U.S. Economic Warfare Provoked Japan's Attack on Pearl Harbor, Independent Institute, 1 May 2006, https://www.independent.org/news/article.asp?id=1930.

29. Tom Rogan, Elbridge Colby: the Brain Behind Trump's Foreign Policy, Unherd, 23 December 2024, https://unherd.com/newsroom/elbridge-colby-the-brain-behind-trumps-foreign-policy/.

30. In the last two Taiwanese presidential elections, a majority supported the pro-independence Democratic Progressive Party, but contemporary public opinion surveys in Taiwan have shown that most respondents favour the status quo but with increasing numbers in recent years backing the combined options of 'maintain the status quo, move towards independence' position, which must be worrisome for Beijing. Only small minorities support immediate independence or unification. Election Study Centre, National Chengchi University, Taiwan Independence vs. Unification with the Mainland (1994/12 – 2022/12), Taipei City/Taiwan, https://esc.nccu.edu.tw/PageDoc/Detail?fid=7801&id=6963; James Lee, Taiwan and the 'New Cold War', Network for Strategic Analysis (NSA), 29 August 2022, https://ras-nsa.ca/taiwan-and-the-new-cold-war/.

CHAPTER 4: REBALANCING THE MIDDLE EAST

1. Steven A. Cook, The End of Ambition: America's Past, Present, and Future in the Middle East, Oxford University Press, 2024.

2. Jake Sullivan, The Sources of American Power. A Foreign Policy for a Changed World, Foreign Affairs, November/December 2023, https://www.foreignaffairs.com/system/files/pdf/2023/FA_102_6_ND2023_Sullivan_print_edition_version.pdf.

3. After the Decapitation of Hizbullah, Iran Could Race For a Nuclear Bomb, The Economist, 30 September 2024, https://www.economist.com/briefing/2024/09/30/iran-could-race-for-the-bomb-after-the-decapitation-of-hizbullah.

4. Maxine Kelly, IAEA Says 'Serious Conversation Due' With Iran Over Nuclear Capabilities, Financial Times, 19 April 2024, https://www.ft.com/content/c6330edb-244d-445c-87cc-e29292d6edda#post-48194b0c-9a94-4340-8532-1216c5eddb30.

5. Ilan Ben Zion, Ex-Israeli Spy Chief: Netanyahu Planned Iran Strike in 2011, Associated Press, 31 May 2018, https://apnews.com/general-news-ff3d8d27040e45f0a24beab254a63e3d.

6. Zach Halaschak, Biden Administration Pushes European Allies Not to

Rebuke Iran Over Nuclear Programme, Washington Examiner, 27 May 2024, https://www.washingtonexaminer.com/policy/foreign-policy/3018452/biden-administration-pushes-european-allies-not-to-rebuke-iran-nuclear-programme/.

7. C. Todd Lopez, Iran Gives Russia Short-Range Missiles, While U.S., Partners Expect to Keep Bolstering Ukrainian Air Defence, DOD News, 10 September 2024, https://www.defence.gov/News/News-Stories/Article/Article/3901774/iran-gives-russia-short-range-missiles-while-us-partners-expect-to-keep-bolster/.

8. Isaac Arnsdorf, Josh Dawsey and Michael Birnbaum, Inside Donald Trump's Secret, Long-shot Plan to End the War in Ukraine, Washington Post, 7 April 2024, https://www.washingtonpost.com/politics/2024/04/05/trump-ukraine-secret-plan/.

9. Christina Lu, How Much Leverage Does China Really Have Over Iran?, Foreign Policy, 19 April 2024, https://foreignpolicy.com/2024/04/19/iran-china-israel-attack-oil-trade-economic-leverage/?tpcc=china_brief&utm_source=Sailthru&utm_medium=email&utm_campaign=China%20Brief%2010012024&utm_term=china_brief.

10. Farnaz Fassihi and Steven Lee Myers, China, With $400 Billion Iran Deal, Could Deepen Influence in Mideast, New York Times, 27 March 2021, https://www.nytimes.com/2021/03/27/world/middleeast/china-iran-deal.html?tpcc=china_brief&utm_source=Sailthru&utm_medium=email&utm_campaign=China%20Brief%2010012024&utm_term=china_brief.

11. Edward Wong, U.S. and Allies Sound Alarm Over Their Adversaries' Military Ties, New York Times, 30 September 2024, https://www.nytimes.com/2024/09/30/us/politics/us-axis-china-iran-russia.html?tpcc=china_brief&utm_source=Sailthru&utm_medium=email&utm_campaign=China%20Brief%2010012024&utm_term=china_brief.

12. David E. Sanger, Candidate Biden Called Saudi Arabia a 'Pariah'. He Now Has to Deal With It, New York Times, 24 February 2021, https://www.nytimes.com/2021/02/24/us/politics/biden-jamal-khashoggi-saudi-arabia.html.

13. Sam Meredith, OPEC+ To Cut Oil Production By 2 Million Barrels Per Day To Shore Up Prices, Defying U.S. Pressure, CNBC, 5 October 2022, https://www.cnbc.com/2022/10/05/oil-opec-imposes-deep-production-cuts-in-a-bid-to-shore-up-prices.html.

CHAPTER 5: GLOBAL SOUTH LEFT OUT
1. Bonnie Bley, A Middle-Power Moment, The Interpreter, Lowry Institute, 23 August 2019, https://www.lowyinstitute.org/the-interpreter/middle-power-moment.

2. Ruchir Sharma, The World Should Take Notice—the Rest are Rising Again, Financial Times, 26 August 2024, https://www.ft.com/content/18cd1c87-

1662-4655-863c-b1cbd378f117.

3. Nicolas Fernandez-Arias, Alberto Musso, Carolina Osorio-Buitron and Adina Popescu, Emerging Markets are Exercising Greater Global Sway, IMF Blog, 9 April 2024, https://www.imf.org/en/Blogs/Articles/2024/04/09/emerging-markets-are-exercising-greater-global-sway.

4. Harvard's Belfer Centre for Science and International Affairs discussed the differentiated impacts of the Covid-19 pandemic on developing countries, highlighting the disadvantages they faced compared to advanced economies. Jeffrey Frankel, The Impact of the Pandemic on Developing Countries, Belfer Centre Blog, 3 August 2020, https://www.belfercentre.org/publication/impact-pandemic-developing-countries. Similarly, the Harvard Kennedy School provided a worrying picture of the impact of the pandemic on developing countries and the medium-term outlook. Jeffrey Frankel, Eliana Carranza, Isabel Guerrero and Rema Hanna, COVID-19: Effects in Developing Countries, Harvard Kennedy School's Dean's Discussions, 22 July 2020, https://www.hks.harvard.edu/more/about/leadership-administration/deans-office/deans-discussions/Covid-19-effects-developing.

5. Michael Singh, The Saudi-Iran Deal Reflects a New Global Reality, Washington Post, 16 March 2023, https://www.washingtonpost.com/opinions/2023/03/16/saudi-arabia-iran-china-deal/.

6. https://x.com/realDonaldTrump/status/1863009545858998512. See also Aime Williams, Trump Threatens Brics Nations with 100% Tariffs If They Undermine Dollar, Financial Times, 30 November 2024, https://www.ft.com/content/18b3d51d-1e4b-4189-bae2-c31248b6526b.

7. Evan Freidin, BRICS Pay As a Challenge to SWIFT Network, The Interpreter, published daily by Australia's Lowry Institute, 13 November 2024, https://www.lowyinstitute.org/the-interpreter/brics-pay-challenge-swift-network.

8. Mohamed El-Erian, Why the West Should Be Paying More Attention To the Gold Price Rise, Financial Times, 21 October 2024, https://www.ft.com/content/b5fb1e6b-bb8d-4ab5-9c92-f1f6fc40a54b.

9. Rowan Scarpino and Jocelyn Trainer, Sanctions by the Numbers: 2023 Year in Review, CNAS, 27 June 2024, https://www.cnas.org/publications/reports/sanctions-by-the-numbers-2023-year-in-review.

10. U.S. Department of Defence, Assistant Secretary of Defence for Indo-Pacific Security Affairs Dr. Ely Ratner Participates in a CNAS Discussion on Building a Networked Security Architecture in the Indo-Pacific, Transcript, 8 June 2023, https://www.defence.gov/News/Transcripts/Transcript/Article/3423120/assistant-secretary-of-defence-for-indo-pacific-security-affairs-dr-ely-ratner/.

11. Kelly A. Grieco and Jennifer Kavanagh, America Can't Surpass China's Power in Asia, Foreign Affairs, 16 January 2024, https://www.foreignaffairs.

com/united-states/america-cant-surpass-chinas-power-asia.

12. Tom Wilson, Russia's Planned Gas Pipeline To China Hit By Construction Delay, Financial Times, 28 January 2024, https://www.ft.com/content/f37f4b84-0d2c-4e7b-882c-3fb26822bb9c.

CHAPTER 6: WAR: NO LONGER UNTHINKABLE

1. Warren P. Strobel, War Game Finds U.S., Taiwan Can Defend Against a Chinese Invasion, The Wall Street Journal, 9 August 2022, https://www.wsj.com/articles/war-game-finds-u-s-taiwan-can-defend-against-a-chinese-invasion-11660047804.

2. Mark D. Kelly quoted in: Stephen Wertheim, World War III Begins With Forgetting, New York Times, 2 December 2022, https://www.nytimes.com/2022/12/02/opinion/america-world-war-iii.html. For more information on the CSIS wargaming, see Justin Katz and Valerie Insinna, 'A bloody Mess' With 'Terrible Loss of Life': How a China-US Conflict Over Taiwan Could Play Out, Breaking Defence, 11 August 2022, https://breakingdefence.com/2022/08/a-bloody-mess-with-terrible-loss-of-life-how-a-china-us-conflict-over-taiwan-could-play-out/.

3. Ibid.

4. Ibid.

5. Ibid.

6. Margaret MacMillan, The War That Ended Peace: The Road to 1914, New York: Random House, 2014.

7. Margaret Macmillan, The Rhyme of History: Lessons of the Great War, Washington, DC: The Brookings Institution, 14 December 2013, http://csweb.brookings.edu/content/research/essays/2013/rhyme-of-history.html.

8. Ibid.

9. Ibid.

10. Charity S. Jacobs and Kathleen M. Carley, Taiwan: China's Grey Zone Doctrine in Action, Small Wars Journal, 11 February 2022, https://smallwarsjournal.com/jrnl/art/taiwan-chinas-grey-zone-doctrine-action.

11. Ibid.

12. Kathrin Hille and Demetri Sevastopulo, US Warns Europe a Conflict Over Taiwan Could Cause Global Economic Shock, Financial Times, 10 November 2022, https://www.ft.com/content/c0b815f3-fd3e-4807-8de7-6b5f72ea8ae5.

13. Kevin Rudd, Rivals Within Reason? U.S.-Chinese Competition Is Getting Sharper – But Doesn't Necessarily Have To Get More Dangerous, Foreign Affairs, 20 July 2022, https://www.foreignaffairs.com/china/rivals-within-reason.

14. Library of America, How Barbara Tuchman's The Guns of August

Influenced Decision Making During the Cuban Missile Crisis, 19 March 2012, https://loa.org/news-and-views/792-how-barbara-tuchmans-_the-guns-of-august_-influenced-decision-making-during-the-cuban-missile-crisis.

15. Maxwell D. Taylor, Swords And Plowshares, New York City, 1972.

16. Michael O'Hanlon, There Should Be No War Over Taiwan, The Hill, 6 September 2022, https://thehill.com/opinion/national-security/3622891-there-should-be-no-war-over-taiwan/.

CHAPTER 7: ENVIRONMENTAL CALAMITY: A VIRTUAL CERTAINTY
1. Copernicus Climate Change Service, Copernicus: 2024 Virtually Certain to Be the Warmest Year and First Year Above 1.5°C, 7 November 2024, https://climate.copernicus.eu/copernicus-2024-virtually-certain-be-warmest-year-and-first-year-above-15degc.

2. Ibid.

3. Will Sullivan, Melting Greenland Ice Sheet Will Cause at Least Ten Inches of Sea-Level Rise, Study Finds, Daily Correspondent, 1 September 2022, https://www.smithsonianmag.com/smart-news/melting-greenland-ice-sheet-will-cause-at-least-ten-inches-of-sea-level-rise-study-finds-180980675/.

4. Marc Jones, Serious Debt Crisis Unfolding Across Developing Countries – UNDP, Reuters, 11 October 2022, https://www.reuters.com/markets/rates-bonds/serious-debt-crisis-unfolding-across-developing-countries-undp-2022-10-11/.

5. United Nations Conference on Trade and Development (UNCTAD), UN Crisis Response Group Calls For Immediate Action To Avert Cascading Impacts of War in Ukraine, 13 April 2022, https://unctad.org/news/un-crisis-response-group-calls-immediate-action-avert-cascading-impacts-war-ukraine.

6. Quoted in: Ben Geman and Andrew Freedman, Kerry: China Tensions Hurting Climate Talks, Axios, 7 March 2023, https://www.axios.com/2023/03/07/john-kerry-us-china-stalled-talks-climate-change.

7. Ole Adolphsen and Jule Könneke, A New Balance Of Power at the 29th World Climate Conference, Stiftung Wissenschaft und Politik, 19 December 2024, https://www.swp-berlin.org/10.18449/2024C57/.

8. Jeff Masters and Bob Henson, The Role of Climate Change in the Catastrophic 2025 Los Angeles Fires, Yale Climate Conditions, https://yaleclimateconnections.org/2025/01/the-role-of-climate-change-in-the-catastrophic-2025-los-angeles-fires/.

9. Niklas Boers quoted in: Damian Carrington, Climate Crisis: Scientists Spot Warning Signs of Gulf Stream Collapse, The Guardian, 5 August 2021, https://www.theguardian.com/environment/2021/aug/05/climate-crisis-scientists-spot-warning-signs-of-gulf-stream-collapse.

10. Ibid.

11. Ibid.

12. Chatham House / Organisation for Security and Co-operation in Europe (OSCE), The Impact of Russia's War Against Ukraine on Climate Security and Climate Action, January 2023, https://alpanalytica.org/wp-content/uploads/2023/02/Independent-Experts-Analysis-The-impact-of-Russias-war-against-Ukraine-on-climate-security-and-climate-action-9-Feb-23.pdf.

13. 'Energy intensity' measures the amount of energy consumed per unit of economic output, often expressed as energy use per unit of GDP. It indicates how efficiently a country or industry uses energy to produce goods and services. Lower energy intensity means higher energy efficiency.

CHAPTER 8: TECHNOLOGY: THE BEST OF TIMES?

1. Ray Kurzweil, The Singularity Is Near: When Humans Transcend Biology, Penguin Books, 2005.

2. Maurice Pitto, Maxime Bleau, Ismaël Djerourou, Samuel Paré, Fabien C Schneider and Daniel-Robert Chebat, Brain-Machine Interfaces To Assist the Blind, Frontiers in Human Neuroscience, 9 February 2021, via National Library of Medicine, https://pmc.ncbi.nlm.nih.gov/articles/PMC7901898/#S2.

3. Mikhail V Blagosklonny, No limit To Maximal Lifespan In Humans: How To Beat a 122-year-old Record, Oncoscience, December 2021, via National Library of Medicine, https://pmc.ncbi.nlm.nih.gov/articles/PMC8636159/#:~:text=Although%20average%20human%20life%20expectancy,morbidity)%2C%20expanding%20morbidity%20span.

4. Selin Oğuz, Visualized: Renewable Energy Capacity Through Time (2000–2023), Decarbonization Channel, 18 June 2024, https://decarbonization.visualcapitalist.com/visualized-renewable-energy-capacity-through-time-2000-2023/.

5. IEA, Renewables 2024, Global Overview, https://www.iea.org/reports/renewables-2024/global-overview.

6. David Keith, What's the Least Bad Way To Cool the Planet?, New York Times, 1 October 2021, https://www.nytimes.com/2021/10/01/opinion/climate-change-geoengineering.html.

7. Ibid.

8. Karen Haoarchive, AI Pioneer Geoff Hinton: 'Deep Learning Is Going To Be Able To Do Everything', MIT Technology Review, 3 November 2020, https://www.technologyreview.com/2020/11/03/1011616/ai-godfather-geoffrey-hinton-deep-learning-will-do-everything/.

9. Will Douglas Heaven, Geoffrey Hinton Tells Us Why He's Now Scared of the Tech He Helped Build, MIT Technology Review, 2 May 2023, https://www.technologyreview.com/2023/05/02/1072528/geoffrey-hinton-google-why-scared-ai/.

10. Henry Kissinger quoted in: David Ignatius, Why Artificial Intelligence Is Now a Primary Concern For Henry Kissinger, Washington Post, 24 November 2022, https://www.washingtonpost.com/opinions/2022/11/24/artificial-intelligence-risk-kissinger-warning-weapons/.

11. Sean Lyngaas, A Record $12.5 Billion in Online Scams Were Reported To the FBI Last Year, CNN, 6 March 2024, https://edition.cnn.com/politics/online-scams-fbi/index.html.

12. The White House, Executive Order on the Safe, Secure, and Trustworthy Development and Use of Artificial Intelligence, 30 October 2023, https://www.whitehouse.gov/briefing-room/presidential-actions/2023/10/30/executive-order-on-the-safe-secure-and-trustworthy-development-and-use-of-artificial-intelligence/.

13. The White House, Memorandum on Advancing the United States' Leadership in Artificial Intelligence; Harnessing Artificial Intelligence to Fulfill National Security Objectives; and Fostering the Safety, Security, and Trustworthiness of Artificial Intelligence, 24 October 2024, https://www.whitehouse.gov/briefing-room/presidential-actions/2024/10/24/memorandum-on-advancing-the-united-states-leadership-in-artificial-intelligence-harnessing-artificial-intelligence-to-fulfill-national-security-objectives-and-fostering-the-safety-security/.

14. Benj Edwards, Trump Allies Want to 'Make America First in AI' with Sweeping Executive Order, Ars Technica, 17 July 2024. https://arstechnica.com/information-technology/2024/07/trump-allies-want-to-make-america-first-in-ai-with-sweeping-executive-order/.

15. Sujai Shivakumar and Charles Wessner, Semiconductors and National Defence: What Are the Stakes?, Centre for Strategic and International Studies (CSIS) Commentary, 8 June 2022, https://www.csis.org/analysis/semiconductors-and-national-defence-what-are-stakes.

16. Ansgar Baums, The 'Chokepoint' Fallacy of Tech Export Controls, Stimson Centre, 6 February 2024, https://www.stimson.org/2024/the-chokepoint-fallacy-of-tech-export-controls/.

17. Madhumita Murgia, Tim Bradshaw, and Richard Waters, Chip Wars With China Risk 'Enormous Damage' to US Tech, Says Nvidia Chief, Financial Times, 24 May 2023, https://www.ft.com/content/ffbb39a8-2eb5-4239-a70e-2e73b9d15f3e.

18. Op. cit. Ansgar Baums, The 'Chokepoint' Fallacy of Tech Export Controls

19. Eleanor Olcott and Zijing Wu, How Small Chinese AI Start-up DeepSeek Shocked Silicon Valley, Financial Times, 27 January 2025, https://www.ft.com/content/747a7b11-dcba-4aa5-8d25-403f56216d7e.

20. Ibid.

21. Ibid.

22. Eric Lipton, As A.I.-Controlled Killer Drones Become Reality, Nations Debate Limits, New York Times, 21 November 2023, https://www.nytimes.com/2023/11/21/us/politics/ai-drones-war-law.html.

23. U.S. Department of Defence, Deputy Secretary of Defence Kathleen Hicks Keynote Address: 'The Urgency to Innovate' (As Delivered), 28 August 2023, https://www.defence.gov/News/Speeches/Speech/Article/3507156/deputy-secretary-of-defence-kathleen-hicks-keynote-address-the-urgency-to-innov/.

24. Michelle Toh, 300 Million Jobs Could Be Affected By Latest Wave of AI, Says Goldman Sachs, CNN, 29 March 2023, https://edition.cnn.com/2023/03/29/tech/chatgpt-ai-automation-jobs-impact-intl-hnk/index.html.

25. Anna Cooban, AI Will Shrink Workforces Within Five Years, Say Company Execs, CNN, 5 April 2024, https://edition.cnn.com/2024/04/05/business/ai-job-losses/index.html.

26. Sarah Schwartz, 'Sharp, Steep Declines': U.S. Students Are Falling Behind in Math and Science Education Week, 4 December 2024, https://www.edweek.org/leadership/sharp-steep-declines-u-s-students-are-falling-behind-in-math-and-science/2024/12.

EPILOGUE: PREPARING FOR A NEW AGE

1. Graham Allison, Destined for War: Can America and China Escape Thucydides's Trap? Houghton Mifflin Harcourt, 2017.

2. Jacob Magid, Blinken: We Assess That Hamas Has Recruited Almost As Many New Fighters As It Has Lost, Times of Israel, 14 January 2025, https://www.timesofisrael.com/liveblog_entry/blinken-we-assess-that-hamas-has-recruited-almost-as-many-new-fighters-as-it-has-lost/.

3. The Biggest Challenge: Everyone Wants More Battery Power, Kantal News, 13 September 2022, https://www.kanthal.com/en/news-stories/news-feed/news-media/2022/september/battery-industry-growth-pains/#:~:text=The%20biggest%20challenge%3A%20everyone%20wants%20more%20battery%20power,rethink%20how%20they%20are%20sourced%2C%20manufactured%20and%20recycled.

4. Plamena Tisheva, China To Reach 1,720 GW Of Solar and Wind By 2025, Says GlobalData, Renewables Now Newsletter, 12 June 2024, https://renewablesnow.com/news/china-to-reach-1-720-gw-of-solar-and-wind-by-2025-says-globaldata-860510/.

5. Steven Dunaway, Global Imbalances and the Financial Crisis, Council on Foreign Relations, March, 2009, https://www.cfr.org/report/global-imbalances-and-financial-crisis.

6. U.S. Department of the Treasury, Remarks by Secretary Henry M. Paulson, Jr., on the Financial Rescue Package and Economic Update, Press Release, 12 November 2008, https://home.treasury.gov/news/press-releases/hp1265.

Bibliography

Adolphsen, Ole and Jule Könneke, A New Balance of Power at the 29th World Climate Conference, Stiftung Wissenschaft und Politik, 19 December 2024, https://www.swp-berlin.org/10.18449/2024C57/.

Allison, Graham, Destined for War: Can America and China Escape Thucydides's Trap? Houghton Mifflin Harcourt, 2017.

Amiti, Mary, Stephen J. Redding and David E. Weinstein, Who's Paying for the US Tariffs? A Longer-Term Perspective, AEA Papers and Proceedings 2020, 110: pp. 541–546, https://doi.org/10.1257/pandp.20201018.

Anderson, Jr., Irvine H., The 1941 De Facto Embargo on Oil to Japan: A Bureaucratic Reflex, Pacific Historical Review (1975) 44 (2): 201–231, https://doi.org/10.2307/3638003.

Arcidiacono, Peter, Josh Kinsler and Tyler Ransom, Legacy and Athlete Preferences at Harvard, National Bureau of Economic Research (NBER) Working Paper Series, No 26316, Cambridge, MA, September 2019, https://www.nber.org/system/files/working_papers/w26316/w26316.pdf.

Arnsdorf, Isaac, Josh Dawsey, and Michael Birnbaum, Inside Donald Trump's Secret, Long-shot Plan to End the War in Ukraine, Washington Post, 7 April 2024, https://www.washingtonpost.com/politics/2024/04/05/trump-ukraine-secret-plan/.

Autor, David H., David Dorn and Gordon H. Hanson, The China Shock:

Learning from Labour Market Adjustment to Large Changes in Trade, National Bureau of Economic Research Working Paper, January 2016, https://www.nber.org/papers/w21906.

Baldwin, Richard, China is the World's Sole Manufacturing Superpower: A Line Sketch of the Rise, CEPR, 17 January 2024, https://cepr.org/voxeu/columns/china-worlds-sole-manufacturing-superpower-line-sketch-rise.

Baums, Ansgar, The 'Chokepoint' Fallacy of Tech Export Controls, Stimson Centre, 6 February 2024, https://www.stimson.org/2024/the-chokepoint-fallacy-of-tech-export-controls/.

Blagosklonny, Mikhail V., No Limit to Maximal Lifespan in Humans: How to Beat a 122-Year-old Record, Oncoscience, December 2021, via National Library of Medicine, https://pmc.ncbi.nlm.nih.gov/articles/PMC8636159/#:~:text=Although%20average%20human%20life%20expectancy,morbidity)%2C%20expanding%20morbidity%20span.

Bley, Bonnie, A Middle-Power Moment, The Interpreter, Lowry Institute, 23 August 2019, https://www.lowyinstitute.org/the-interpreter/middle-power-moment.

Bokat-Lindell, Spencer, Should We Block the Sun to Counter Climate Change?, New York Times, 11 January 2023, https://www.nytimes.com/2023/01/11/opinion/geoengineering-climate-change-solar.html.

Burguete, Víctor, China and the Global South: Trade, Investment and Rescue Loans, Barcelona Centre for International Affairs, November 2023, https://www.cidob.org/en/publications/china-and-global-south-trade-investment-and-rescue-loans.

Burrows, Mathew, European Security Post-Ukraine War, Stimson Policy Memo, 9 August 2024, https://www.stimson.org/2024/european-security-post-ukraine-war/.

Carrington, Damian, Climate Crisis: Scientists Spot Warning Signs of Gulf Stream Collapse, The Guardian, 5 August 2021, https://www.theguardian.com/environment/2021/aug/05/climate-crisis-scientists-spot-warning-signs-of-gulf-stream-collapse.

Carville, James, I Was Wrong About the 2024 Election. Here's Why, New York Times, 2 January 2025, https://www.nytimes.com/2025/01/02/opinion/democrats-donald-trump-economy.html?searchResultPosition=1.

Chaffin, Joshua and Deborah Acosta, How a Real Estate Mogul Became Trump's Middle East Point Man, Wall Street Journal, 17 November 2024, https://www.wsj.com/politics/elections/trump-transition-witkoff-middle-east-39364c30?mod=hp_lead_pos8.

Chang, Agnes and Keith Bradsher, Can the World Make an Electric Car Battery Without China?, New York Times, 16 May 2023, https://www.nytimes.com/interactive/2023/05/16/business/china-ev-battery.html?searchResultPosition=2.

Charap, Samuel, and Sergey Radchenko, The Talks That Could Have Ended the War in Ukraine. A Hidden History of Diplomacy That Came Up Short—But Holds Lessons for Future Negotiations, in Foreign Affairs, 16 April 2024, https://www.foreignaffairs.com/ukraine/talks-could-have-ended-war-ukraine.

Chatham House / Organisation for Security and Co-operation in Europe (OSCE), The Impact of Russia's War Against Ukraine on Climate Security and Climate Action, January 2023, https://alpanalytica.org/wp-content/uploads/2023/02/Independent-Experts-Analysis-The-impact-of-Russias-war-against-Ukraine-on-climate-security-and-climate-action-9-Feb-23.pdf.

China Daily, Xi Sets Targets for China's Science, Technology Progress, 30 May 2016, https://www.chinadaily.com.cn/china/2016-05/30/content_25540484.htm.

Committee for a Responsible Federal Budget, Analysis of CBO's March 2024 Long-Term Budget Outlook, 20 March 2024, https://www.crfb.org/papers/analysis-cbos-march-2024-long-term-budget-outlook.

Congressional Budget Office (CBO), Climate Change, https://www.cbo.gov/topics/climate-and-environment/climate-change.

Cooban, Anna, AI Will Shrink Workforces Within Five Years, Say Company Execs, CNN, 5 April 2024, https://edition.cnn.com/2024/04/05/business/ai-job-losses/index.html.

Cook, Steven A., The End of Ambition: America's Past, Present, and Future in the Middle East, Oxford University Press, 2024.

Copernicus Climate Change Service (C3S), Copernicus: 2024 Virtually Certain to Be the Warmest Year and First Year Above 1.5°C, 7 November 2024, https://climate.copernicus.eu/copernicus-2024-virtually-certain-be-warmest-year-and-first-year-above-15degc.

Deal, Jacqueline, Trump, Congress Must Fix the National Emergency that

Biden Declared, The Hill, 9 December 2024, https://thehill.com/opinion/5029506-biden-executive-order-china-technology/.

DeFusco, Jackie, Trump Backs Foreign Worker Visa Programme Splitting His Supporters, WDSU, 29 December 2024, https://www.wdsu.com/article/trump-h1b-visa-debate/63299446.

De Soyres, Francois and Dylan Moore, Assessing China's Efforts to Increase Self-Reliance, FEDS Notes, Federal Reserve of the United States, 2 February 2024, https://www.federalreserve.gov/econres/notes/feds-notes/assessing-chinas-efforts-to-increase-self-reliance-20240202.html.

Dizikes, Peter, Q&A: David Autor on the Long Afterlife of the 'China Shock', MIT News, 6 December 2021, https://news.mit.edu/2021/david-autor-china-shock-persists-1206.

Douglas, Jason, China Has Limited Firepower to Counter U.S. Tariffs, Wall Street Journal, 29 December 2024, https://www.wsj.com/economy/trade/china-has-limited-firepower-to-counter-u-s-tariffs-108df7e9?page=1.

Dunaway, Steven, Global Imbalances and the Financial Crisis, Council on Foreign Relations, March, 2009, https://www.cfr.org/report/global-imbalances-and-financial-crisis.

Economist, After the Decapitation of Hizbullah, Iran Could Race for a Nuclear Bomb, 30 September 2024, https://www.economist.com/briefing/2024/09/30/iran-could-race-for-the-bomb-after-the-decapitation-of-hizbullah.

Edwards, Benj, Trump Allies Want to 'Make America First in AI' With Sweeping Executive Order, Ars Technica, 17 July 2024, https://arstechnica.com/information-technology/2024/07/trump-allies-want-to-make-america-first-in-ai-with-sweeping-executive-order/.

Election Study Centre, National Chengchi University, Taiwan Independence vs. Unification with the Mainland (1994/12 – 2022/12), Taipei City/Taiwan, https://esc.nccu.edu.tw/PageDoc/Detail?fid=7801&id=6963.

El-Erian, Mohamed, Why the West Should Be Paying More Attention to the Gold Price Rise, Financial Times, 21 October 2024, https://www.ft.com/content/b5fb1e6b-bb8d-4ab5-9c92-f1f6fc40a54b.

Fassihi, Farnaz and Steven Lee Myers, China, With $400 Billion Iran Deal, Could Deepen Influence in Mideast, New York Times, 27 March 2021, https://www.nytimes.com/2021/03/27/world/middleeast/china-iran-deal.

html?tpcc=china_brief&utm_source=Sailthru&utm_medium=email&utm_campaign=China%20Brief%2010012024&utm_term=china_brief.

Ferguson, Niall and Moritz Schularick, The End of Chimerica, Harvard Business School Working Paper, No. 10-037, November 2009.

Fernandez-Arias, Nicolas, Alberto Musso, Carolina Osorio-Buitron and Adina Popescu, Emerging Markets are Exercising Greater Global Sway, IMF Blog, 9 April 2024, https://www.imf.org/en/Blogs/Articles/2024/04/09/emerging-markets-are-exercising-greater-global-sway.

Frankel, Jeffrey, The Impact of the Pandemic on Developing Countries, Belfer Centre Blog, 3 August 2020, https://www.belfercentre.org/publication/impact-pandemic-developing-countries.

Frankel, Jeffrey, Eliana Carranza, Isabel Guerrero and Rema Hanna, COVID-19: Effects in Developing Countries, Harvard Kennedy School's Dean's Discussions, 22 July 2020, https://www.hks.harvard.edu/more/about/leadership-administration/deans-office/deans-discussions/covid-19-effects-developing.

Freidin, Evan, BRICS Pay As a Challenge to SWIFT Network, The Interpreter, published daily by Australia's Lowry Institute, 13 November 2024, https://www.lowyinstitute.org/the-interpreter/brics-pay-challenge-swift-network.

Friedman, Lisa, Biden Bans New Oil and Gas Drilling Along Most U.S. Coasts, New York Times, 6 January 2025, https://www.nytimes.com/2025/01/06/climate/biden-oil-gas-drilling-ban.html?searchResultPosition=2.

Gardner, Timothy, Biden Pauses LNG Export Approvals After Pressure From Climate Activists, in: Reuters, 26 January 2024, https://www.reuters.com/business/energy/biden-pauses-approval-new-lng-export-projects-win-climate-activists-2024-01-26/

Geman. Ben and Andrew Freedman, Kerry: China Tensions Hurting Climate Talks, Axios, 7 March 2023, https://www.axios.com/2023/03/07/john-kerry-us-china-stalled-talks-climate-change.

Ghosh, Iman, How China Overtook the US and the World's Major Trading Partner, Visual Capitalist, 22 January 2020, https://www.visualcapitalist.com/china-u-s-worlds-trading-partner/#:~:text=How%20China%20Overtook%20the%20U.S.%20as%20the%20World%E2%80%99s%20Major%20Trading%20Partner.

Gillam, Laura H. and Wesley E. Yin, Responding to the Financial Impacts of Climate Change, The White House, Office of Management and Budget (OMB), 22 April 2024, https://www.whitehouse.gov/omb/briefing-room/2024/04/22/responding-to-the-financial-impacts-of-climate-change/.

Global Times, GT Yearender: China Stands Firm Against Relentless US Crackdown in 2022, 29 December 2022, https://www.globaltimes.cn/page/202212/1282912.shtml.

Grabow, Colin, Inflation Another Reason to Rethink Buy American Protectionism, Cato at Liberty Blog, 20 April 2022, https://www.cato.org/blog/touting-buy-american-protectionism-inflation-antidote-economic-quackery.

Grieco, Kelly A. and Jennifer Kavanagh, America Can't Surpass China's Power in Asia, Foreign Affairs, 16 January 2024, https://www.foreignaffairs.com/united-states/america-cant-surpass-chinas-power-asia.

Guliyev, Farid, Trump's 'America first' Energy Policy, Contingency and the Reconfiguration of the Global Energy Order, Energy Policy, Vol 140, May 2020, https://doi.org/10.1016/j.enpol.2020.11143.

Halaschak, Zach, Biden Administration Pushes European Allies Not to Rebuke Iran Over Nuclear Programme, Washington Examiner, 27 May 2024, https://www.washingtonexaminer.com/policy/foreign-policy/3018452/biden-administration-pushes-european-allies-not-to-rebuke-iran-nuclear-programme/

Haoarchive, Karen, AI Pioneer Geoff Hinton: Deep Learning Is Going to Be Able to Do Everything, MIT Technology Review, 3 November 2020, https://www.technologyreview.com/2020/11/03/1011616/ai-godfather-geoffrey-hinton-deep-learning-will-do-everything/.

Heaven, Will Douglas, Geoffrey Hinton Tells Us Why He's Now Scared of the Tech He Helped Build, MIT Technology Review, 2 May 2023, https://www.technologyreview.com/2023/05/02/1072528/geoffrey-hinton-google-why-scared-ai/

Helenjak, Timothy, Eeva Turunen and Shinan Wang, Cities on Ice: Population Change in Arctic, Nordregio Magazine, https://nordregio.org/nordregio-magazine/issues/arctic-changes-and-challenges/cities-on-ice-population-change-in-the-arctic/

Higgs, Robert, How U.S. Economic Warfare Provoked Japan's Attack on Pearl Harbor, Independent Institute, 1 May 2006, https://www.

independent.org/news/article.asp?id=1930.

Hille, Kathrin and Demetri Sevastopulo, US Warns Europe a Conflict Over Taiwan Could Cause Global Economic Shock, Financial Times, 10 November 2022, https://www.ft.com/content/c0b815f3-fd3e-4807-8de7-6b5f72ea8ae5.

Hodge, Nathan, The CIA Chief Says Putin Is 'Entirely Too Healthy'. What Do We Really Know About His Condition?, CNN, 21 July 2022, https://www.cnn.com/2022/07/21/europe/vladimir-putin-health-cia-cmd-intl/index.html.

Hoffman, Jon, Time Is Running Out For Iran-US Diplomacy. Trump Should Strike a Deal With Iran, The Hill, 30 December 2024, https://thehill.com/opinion/5059043-trump-diplomacy-iran-nuclear/

Hufbauer, Gary Clyde, Megan Hogan and Yilin Wang, For Inflation Relief, the United States Should Look to Trade Liberalization, Peterson Institute for International Economics (PIIE) Policy Brief, March 2022, https://www.piie.com/sites/default/files/documents/pb22-4.pdf.

Ignatius, David, Why Artificial Intelligence Is Now a Primary Concern for Henry Kissinger, Washington Post, 24 November 2022, https://www.washingtonpost.com/opinions/2022/11/24/artificial-intelligence-risk-kissinger-warning-weapons/

International Energy Agency (IEA), Renewables 2024, Global Overview, https://www.iea.org/reports/renewables-2024/global-overview.

Jackson, Brooks, Eugene Kiely, D'Angelo Gore, Lori Robertson and Robert Farley, Biden's Numbers, July 2024 Update, Annenberg Public Policy Centre, FactCheck.org, 25 July 2024, https://www.factcheck.org/2024/07/bidens-numbers-july-2024-update/

Jacobs, Charity S. and Kathleen M. Carley, Taiwan: China's Grey Zone Doctrine in Action, Small Wars Journal, 11 February 2022, https://smallwarsjournal.com/jrnl/art/taiwan-chinas-grey-zone-doctrine-action.

Jacobs, Jennifer, and Peter Martin, Trump Eyes NATO Makeover, Hurried Peace in Ukraine If Elected, Bloomberg, 14 February 2024, https://www.bloomberg.com/news/articles/2024-02-14/trump-eyes-two-tier-nato-security-pledge-zelenskiy-putin-peace-talks-if-elected.

Johnson, Christopher, Why China Will Play It Safe, Foreign Affairs, 14 November 2022, https://www.foreignaffairs.com/china/why-china-will-play-it-safe.

Jones, Marc, Serious Debt Crisis Unfolding Across Developing Countries – UNDP, Reuters, 11 October 2022, https://www.reuters.com/markets/rates-bonds/serious-debt-crisis-unfolding-across-developing-countries-undp-2022-10-11/

Kantal News, The Biggest Challenge: Everyone Wants More Battery Power, 13 September 2022, https://www.kanthal.com/en/news-stories/news-feed/news-media/2022/september/battery-industry-growth-pains/#:~:text=The%20biggest%20challenge%3A%20everyone%20wants%20more%20battery%20power,rethink%20how%20they%20are%20sourced%2C%20manufactured%20and%20recycled.

Keith, David, What's the Least Bad Way to Cool the Planet?, New York Times, 1 October 2021, https://www.nytimes.com/2021/10/01/opinion/climate-change-geoengineering.html.

Kelly, Maxine, IAEA Says 'Serious Conversation Due' With Iran Over Nuclear Capabilities, Financial Times, 19 April 2024, https://www.ft.com/content/c6330edb-244d-445c-87cc-e29292d6edda#post-48194b0c-9a94-4340-8532-1216c5eddb30.

Kennedy, Brian and Alec Tyson, How Republicans View Climate Change and Energy Issues, Pew Research Centre, 1 March 2024, https://www.pewresearch.org/short-reads/2024/03/01/how-republicans-view-climate-change-and-energy-issues/

Kurzweil, Ray, The Singularity Is Near: When Humans Transcend Biology, Penguin Books, 2005.

Lee, James, Taiwan and the 'New Cold War', Network for Strategic Analysis (NSA), 29 August 2022, https://ras-nsa.ca/taiwan-and-the-new-cold-war/

Liboreiro, Josep Jorge, Borrell Apologises For Controversial 'Garden Vs Jungle' Metaphor But Defends Speech, Euronews, 19 October 2022, https://www.euronews.com/my-europe/2022/10/19/josep-borrell-apologises-for-controversial-garden-vs-jungle-metaphor-but-stands-his-ground.

Library of America, How Barbara Tuchman's the Guns of August Influenced Decision Making During the Cuban Missile Crisis, 19 March 2012, https://loa.org/news-and-views/792-how-barbara-tuchmans-_the-guns-of-august_-influenced-decision-making-during-the-cuban-missile-crisis.

Lincicome, Scott, Grading Trump's Economic Policies, Cato Commentary, Cato Institute, 16 October 2020, https://www.cato.org/commentary/

grading-trumps-economic-policies#.

Lipton, Eric, As A.I.-Controlled Killer Drones Become Reality, Nations Debate Limits, New York Times, 21 November 2023, https://www.nytimes.com/2023/11/21/us/politics/ai-drones-war-law.html.

Litvinov, Amanda, Three Years In, Biden's American Rescue Plan Buoys Millions of Students and Educators, NEA Today, 11 March 2024, https://www.nea.org/nea-today/all-news-articles/three-years-bidens-american-rescue-plan-buoys-millions-students-and-educators.

Longworth, Philip, Russia's Empires: Their Rise and Fall From Prehistory to Putin, London: John Murray, 2006.

Lopez, C. Todd, Iran Gives Russia Short-Range Missiles, While U.S., Partners Expect to Keep Bolstering Ukrainian Air Defence, DOD News, 10 September 2024, https://www.defence.gov/News/News-Stories/Article/Article/3901774/iran-gives-russia-short-range-missiles-while-us-partners-expect-to-keep-bolster/.

Lu, Christina, How Much Leverage Does China Really Have Over Iran?, Foreign Policy, 19 April 2024, https://foreignpolicy.com/2024/04/19/iran-china-israel-attack-oil-trade-economic-leverage/?tpcc=china_brief&utm_source=Sailthru&utm_medium=email&utm_campaign=China%20Brief%2010012024&utm_term=china_brief.

Luce, Edward, Containing China Is Biden's Explicit Goal, Financial Times, 19 October 2022, https://www.ft.com/content/398f0d4e-906e-479b-a9a7-e4023c298f39.

Lyngaas, Sean, A record $12.5 Billion in Online Scams Were Reported to the FBI Last Year, CNN, 6 March 2024, https://edition.cnn.com/politics/online-scams-fbi/index.html.

Lyons, Patrick J., Isabelle Taft and Eileen Sullivan, Trump Plans to Put an End to Birthright Citizenship. That Could Be Hard, New York Times, 20 January 2025, https://www.nytimes.com/2025/01/20/us/politics/can-trump-end-birthright-citizenship-not-easily.html?searchResultPosition=2.

MacMillan, Margaret, The Rhyme of History: Lessons of the Great War, Washington, DC: The Brookings Institution, 14 December 2013, http://csweb.brookings.edu/content/research/essays/2013/rhyme-of-history.html.

MacMillan, Margaret, The War That Ended Peace: The Road to 1914, New York: Random House, 2014.

MacMillan, Margaret, Stress Test: Can a Troubled Order Survive a Disruptive Leader?, Foreign Affairs, January/February 2025, Published on 7 January 2025, https://www.foreignaffairs.com/united-states/stress-test-trump-margaret-macmillan.

Martin, Marc S., Meeka Bondy and Sydney Veatch, What to Expect From the Trump Administration on AI Policy, PerkinCoi, 5 December 2024, https://perkinscoie.com/insights/update/what-expect-trump-administration-ai-policy.

Masters, Jeff and Bob Henson, The Role of Climate Change in the Catastrophic 2025 Los Angeles Fires, Yale Climate Conditions, https://yaleclimateconnections.org/2025/01/the-role-of-climate-change-in-the-catastrophic-2025-los-angeles-fires/.

McBride, James and Andrew Chatzky, Is 'Made in China 2025' a Threat to Global Trade?, Council on Foreign Relations (CFR) Backgrounder, 13 May 2019, https://www.cfr.org/backgrounder/made-china-2025-threat-global-trade.

McIntyre, Jamie, Vance Says Trump's Plan to End the War Would Likely Force Ukraine to Give Up Land, NATO Aspirations, Washington Examiner, 13 September 2024, https://www.msn.com/en-us/news/world/vance-says-trump-s-plan-to-end-the-war-would-likely-force-ukraine-to-give-up-land-nato-aspirations/ar-AA1qvNSS.

McKibbin, Warwick J., Megan Hogan and Marcus Noland, The International Economic Implications of a Second Trump Presidency, Peterson Institute for International Economics (PIIE) Working Papers 24-20, September 2024, https://www.piie.com/publications/working-papers/2024/international-economic-implications-second-trump-presidency.

Menasce Horowitz, Juliana, Ruth Igielnik and Rakesh Kochhar, Trends in Income and Wealth Inequality, Pew Research Centre, 9 January 2020, https://www.pewresearch.org/social-trends/2020/01/09/trends-in-income-and-wealth-inequality/.

Meredith, Sam, OPEC+ To Cut Oil Production By 2 Million Barrels Per Day To Shore Up Prices, Defying U.S. Pressure, CNBC, 5 October 2022, https://www.cnbc.com/2022/10/05/oil-opec-imposes-deep-production-cuts-in-a-bid-to-shore-up-prices.html.

Milanović, Branko, The Ideology of Donald J. Trump, Global Inequality and More 3.0 Blog, 12 November 2024, https://

branko2f7.substack.com/p/the-ideology-of-donald-j-trump?utm_source=substack&publication_id=371309&post_id=151536896&utm_medium=email&utm_content=share&utm_campaign=email-share&triggerShare=true&isFreemail=true&r=1u308u&triedRedirect=true.

Milanović, Branko, How the Mainstream Abandoned Universal Economic Principles (But Forgot to Mention It), Global Inequality and More 3.0 Blog, 8 January 2025, https://branko2f7.substack.com/p/how-the-mainstream-has-abandoned?utm_source=post-email-title&publication_id=371309&post_id=154385191&utm_campaign=email-post-title&isFreemail=true&r=1u308u&triedRedirect=true&utm_medium=email.

Moyer, Jonathan D., Collin J. Meisel, Austin S. Matthews, David K. Bohl, and Mathew J. Burrows, China-US Competition: Measuring Global Influence, Atlantic Council, Washington, DC, May 2021, https://www.atlanticcouncil.org/wp-content/uploads/2021/06/China-US-Competition-Report-2021.pdf.

Murgia, Madhumita, Tim Bradshaw and Richard Waters, Chip Wars With China Risk 'Enormous Damage' to US Tech, Says Nvidia Chief, Financial Times, 24 May 2023, https://www.ft.com/content/ffbb39a8-2eb5-4239-a70e-2e73b9d15f3e.

Nagle, Molly and Kelsey Walsh, Administration Official Shares Inside Story of How Hamas-Israel Deal Came About, ABCNews, 15 January 2025, https://abcnews.go.com/Politics/white-house-official-shares-inside-story-hamas-israel/story?id=117723507.

Narea, Nicole, Biden Isn't Advertising America's Record Oil Boom, Vox, 13 March 2024, https://www.vox.com/climate/24098983/biden-oil-production-climate-fossil-fuel-renewables.

NBC News, Greenspan Admits 'Mistake' That Helped Crisis, 23 October 2008, https://www.nbcnews.com/id/wbna27335454.

Obstfeld, Maurice, Jay Shambaugh and Alan Taylor, Financial Instability, Reserves, and Central Bank Swap Lines in the Panic of 2008, Paper Presented at the ASSA Meetings, January 2009, American Economic Review, Papers and Proceedings, p. 30.

Oğuz, Selin, Visualized: Renewable Energy Capacity Through Time (2000–2023), Decarbonization Channel, 18 June 2024, https://decarbonization.visualcapitalist.com/visualized-renewable-energy-capacity-through-time-2000-2023/.

O'Hanlon, Michael, There Should Be No War Over Taiwan, The Hill, 6 September 2022, https://thehill.com/opinion/national-security/3622891-there-should-be-no-war-over-taiwan/.

Page Fortna, Virginia, Does Peacekeeping Work? Shaping Belligerents' Choices After Civil War, Princeton University Press, 2008.

Pettis, Michael, China's Great Demand Challenge, Far Eastern Economic Review, January 2009, pp. 8-13.

Pitto, Maurice, Maxime Bleau, Ismaël Djerourou, Samuel Paré, Fabien C Schneider and Daniel-Robert Chebat, Brain-Machine Interfaces to Assist the Blind, Frontiers in Human Neuroscience, 9 February 2021, via National Library of Medicine, https://pmc.ncbi.nlm.nih.gov/articles/PMC7901898/#S2.

Posen, Adam S., The Price of Nostalgia. America's Self-Defeating Economic Retreat, Foreign Affairs, May/June 2021, published on 20 April 2021, https://www.foreignaffairs.com/articles/united-states/2021-04-20/america-price-nostalgia.

Rampell, Catherine, A 'War on American Energy'? So Why Is Oil Production Near Record Highs?, Washington Post, 3 October 2023, https://www.washingtonpost.com/opinions/2023/10/03/biden-fossil-fuels-republicans-energy-war-record/.

Rascoe, Ayesha, The Racial Income Gap Has Narrowed for Black Americans, New Research Shows, NPR, 4 August 2024, https://www.npr.org/2024/08/04/nx-s1-5059187/the-racial-income-gap-has-narrowed-for-black-americans-new-research-shows.

Ravid, Barak and David Lawler, Scoop: Denmark Sent Trump Team Private Messages on Greenland, Axios, 11 January 2025, https://www.axios.com/2025/01/11/denmark-response-trump-greenland-threat.

Reisen, Helmut, Shifting Wealth: Is the U.S. Dollar Empire Falling?, VoxEu.org, 20 June 2009, https://cepr.org/voxeu/columns/shifting-wealth-us-dollar-empire-falling.

Reuters / US News, Iran's President Says Tehran Has to Deal With Washington, 12 November 2024, https://www.usnews.com/news/world/articles/2024-11-12/iran-says-it-will-pursue-its-interest-when-asked-about-possibility-of-trump-talks.

Roper Centre for Public Opinion Research, 22 June 2015, https://ropercentre.cornell.edu/blog/seventy-years-us-public-opinion-united-nations.

Rudd, Kevin, Rivals Within Reason? U.S.-Chinese Competition Is Getting Sharper – But Doesn't Necessarily Have to Get More Dangerous, Foreign Affairs, 20 July 2022, https://www.foreignaffairs.com/china/rivals-within-reason.

Ryan, Carol, OPEC Cartel Has Nothing on China's Clean-Energy Monopoly, Wall Street Journal, 16 January 2023, https://www.wsj.com/articles/opec-cartel-has-nothing-on-chinas-clean-energy-monopoly-11673883488.

Sainato, Michael, 'They Would Not Listen to Us': Inside Arizona's Troubled Chip Plant, The Guardian, 28 August 28, 2023, https://www.theguardian.com/business/2023/aug/28/phoenix-microchip-plant-biden-union-tsmc.

Sanger, David E., Candidate Biden Called Saudi Arabia a 'Pariah'. He Now Has to Deal With It, New York Times, 24 February 2021, https://www.nytimes.com/2021/02/24/us/politics/biden-jamal-khashoggi-saudi-arabia.html.

Scarpino, Rowan and Jocelyn Trainer, Sanctions by the Numbers: 2023 Year in Review, CNAS, 27 June 2024, https://www.cnas.org/publications/reports/sanctions-by-the-numbers-2023-year-in-review.

Schwartz, Sarah, 'Sharp, Steep Declines': U.S. Students Are Falling Behind in Math and Science, Education Week, 4 December 2024, https://www.edweek.org/leadership/sharp-steep-declines-u-s-students-are-falling-behind-in-math-and-science/2024/12.

Segal, Edward, How a Mass Deportation of Immigrants Would Impact Businesses, Forbes, 18 November 2024, https://www.forbes.com/sites/edwardsegal/2024/11/17/how-a-mass-deportation-of-immigrants-could-impact-businesses/.

Sharma, Ruchir, The World Should Take Notice—The Rest Are Rising Again, Financial Times, 26 August 2024, https://www.ft.com/content/18cd1c87-1662-4655-863c-b1cbd378f117.

Shivakumar, Sujai and Charles Wessner, Semiconductors and National Defence: What Are the Stakes?, Centre for Strategic and International Studies (CSIS) Commentary, 8 June 2022, https://www.csis.org/analysis/semiconductors-and-national-defence-what-are-stakes.

Singh, Michael, The Saudi-Iran Deal Reflects a New Global Reality, Washington Post, 16 March 2023, https://www.washingtonpost.com/opinions/2023/03/16/saudi-arabia-iran-china-deal/.

Slav, Irina, China and India Account for More Than 90% of Russian Oil and Fuel Exports, Oilprice.com, 27 December 2023, https://oilprice.com/Latest-Energy-News/World-News/China-and-India-Account-for-More-Than-90-of-Russian-Oil-and-Fuel-Exports.html.

Smeltz, Dina, Lama El Baz and Denis Volkov, Russians More Interested in Peace Talks with Ukraine, But Most Oppose Making Major Concessions, Chicago Council on Global Affairs, 9 October 2024, https://globalaffairs.org/research/public-opinion-survey/russians-more-interested-peace-talks-ukraine-most-oppose-making.

Strobel, Warren P., War Game Finds U.S., Taiwan Can Defend Against a Chinese Invasion, The Wall Street Journal, 9 August 2022, https://www.wsj.com/articles/war-game-finds-u-s-taiwan-can-defend-against-a-chinese-invasion-11660047804.

Suebsaeng, Asawin and Andrew Perez, Team Trump Debates How Much Should We Invade Mexico, Rolling Stone, 27 November 2024, https://www.rollingstone.com/politics/politics-features/trump-mexico-drug-cartels-military-invade-1235183177/.

Sullivan, Jake, The Sources of American Power. A Foreign Policy for a Changed World, Foreign Affairs, November/December 2023, https://www.foreignaffairs.com/system/files/pdf/2023/FA_102_6_ND2023_Sullivan_print_edition_version.pdf.

Svetlova, Ksenia, How Iraq became the Top Link in China's Belt and Road Strategy, The Media Line, 6 February 2022, https://themedialine.org/top-stories/how-iraq-became-the-top-link-in-beijings-belt-and-road-strategy/

Tang, Didi, Trump Says Taiwan Should Pay More For Defence And Dodges Questions If He Would Defend the Island, Associated Press, 18 July 2024, https://apnews.com/article/trump-taiwan-chips-invasion-china-910e7a94b19248fc75e5d1ab6b0a34d8.

Tang, Didi, China's Xi Is Likely to Decline Trump's Inauguration Invitation, Seeing It As Too Risky to Attend, The Hill, 24 December 2024, https://thehill.com/homenews/ap/ap-international/ap-chinas-xi-is-likely-to-decline-trumps-inauguration-invitation-seeing-it-as-too-risky-to-attend/.

Taylor, Maxwell D., Swords and Plowshares, New York City, 1972.

Tisheva, Plamena, China to Reach 1,720 GW of Solar and Wind by 2025, Says GlobalData, Renewables Now Newsletter, 12 June 2024, https://

renewablesnow.com/news/china-to-reach-1-720-gw-of-solar-and-wind-by-2025-says-globaldata-860510/.

Toh, Michelle, 300 Million Jobs Could Be Affected by Latest Wave of AI, says Goldman Sachs, CNN, 29 March 2023, https://edition.cnn.com/2023/03/29/tech/chatgpt-ai-automation-jobs-impact-intl-hnk/index.html.

Trethart, Albert and Olivia Case, Do People Trust the UN? A Look at the Data, 22 February 2023 https://theglobalobservatory.org/2023/02/do-people-trust-the-un-a-look-at-the-data/.

Trump, Donald, Agenda47: Preventing World War III, 16 March 2023, https://www.donaldjtrump.com/agenda47/agenda47-preventing-world-war-iii.

Trump, Donald, @realDonaldTrump, https://x.com/realDonaldTrump/status/1863009545858998512.

Trump, Donald, Second Inaugural Speech, Annotated, New York Times, 20 January 2025, https://www.nytimes.com/interactive/2025/01/20/us/trump-inauguration-speech-annotated.html.

Unherd, Tom Rogan and Elbridge Colby: The Brain Behind Trump's Foreign Policy, 23 December 2024, https://unherd.com/newsroom/elbridge-colby-the-brain-behind-trumps-foreign-policy/.

United Nations Conference on Trade and Development (UNCTAD), UN Crisis Response Group Calls For Immediate Action to Avert Cascading Impacts of War in Ukraine, 13 April 2022, https://unctad.org/news/un-crisis-response-group-calls-immediate-action-avert-cascading-impacts-war-ukraine.

United Nations Environmental Programmeme, Emissions Gap Report 2023, 20 November 2023, https://www.unep.org/resources/emissions-gap-report-2023.

U.S. Census Bureau, Opportunity Atlas, https://www.census.gov/library/stories/2018/10/opportunity-atlas.html.

U.S. Department of Defence, Assistant Secretary of Defence for Indo-Pacific Security Affairs Dr. Ely Ratner Participates in a CNAS Discussion on Building a Networked Security Architecture in the Indo-Pacific, Transcript, 8 June 2023, https://www.defence.gov/News/Transcripts/Transcript/Article/3423120/assistant-secretary-of-defence-for-indo-pacific-security-affairs-dr-ely-ratner/.

U.S. Department of Defence, Deputy Secretary of Defence Kathleen Hicks Keynote Address: 'The Urgency to Innovate' (As Delivered), 28 August 2023, https://www.defence.gov/News/Speeches/Speech/Article/3507156/deputy-secretary-of-defence-kathleen-hicks-keynote-address-the-urgency-to-innov/.

U.S. Department of the Treasury, Fiscal Data, https://fiscaldata.treasury.gov/americas-finance-guide/national-debt/.

U.S. Department of the Treasury, Remarks by Secretary Henry M. Paulson, Jr., on the Financial Rescue Package and Economic Update, Press Release, 12 November 2008.

U.S. Energy Information Administration (EIA), Arctic Oil and Natural Gas Resources, 20 January 2012, https://www.eia.gov/todayinenergy/detail.php?id=4650.

U.S. Government Accountability Office, International Infrastructure Projects: China's Investments Significantly Outpace the U.S., and Experts Suggest Potential Improvements to the U.S. Approach, 12 September 2024, https://www.gao.gov/products/gao-24-106866#:~:text=What GAO Found. From 2013 to 2021%2C,provided $76 billion in the same sectors.

Vahlsing, Candace and Zach Liscow, The Importance of Measuring the Fiscal and Economic Costs of Climate Change, The White House, Office of Management and Budget (OMB), 14 March 2023, https://www.whitehouse.gov/omb/briefing-room/2023/03/14/the-importance-of-measuring-the-fiscal-and-economic-costs-of-climate-change/

Vickers, Clayton, Trump Defends NATO Threats As 'a Form of Negotiation', in: The Hill, 19 March 2024, https://thehill.com/policy/international/4542440-trump-defends-nato-threats-as-a-form-of-negotiation/

Wertheim, Stephen, WWIII Begins With Forgetting, New York Times, 2 December 2022, https://www.nytimes.com/2022/12/02/opinion/america-world-war-iii.html.

White House, Executive Order on the Safe, Secure, and Trustworthy Development and Use of Artificial Intelligence, 30 October 2023, https://www.whitehouse.gov/briefing-room/presidential-actions/2023/10/30/executive-order-on-the-safe-secure-and-trustworthy-development-and-use-of-artificial-intelligence/

White House, Biden-Harris Administration Announces Temporary Pause on Pending Approvals of Liquefied Natural Gas Exports, Fact Sheet, Washington, DC, 26 January 2024, https://www.whitehouse.gov/briefing-room/statements-releases/2024/01/26/fact-sheet-biden-harris-administration-announces-temporary-pause-on-pending-approvals-of-liquefied-natural-gas-exports/

White House, Memorandum on Advancing the United States' Leadership in Artificial Intelligence; Harnessing Artificial Intelligence to Fulfill National Security Objectives; and Fostering the Safety, Security, and Trustworthiness of Artificial Intelligence, 24 October 2024, https://www.whitehouse.gov/briefing-room/presidential-actions/2024/10/24/memorandum-on-advancing-the-united-states-leadership-in-artificial-intelligence-harnessing-artificial-intelligence-to-fulfill-national-security-objectives-and-fostering-the-safety-security/

Williams, Aime, Trump Threatens Brics Nations with 100% Tariffs If They Undermine Dollar, Financial Times, 30 November 2024, https://www.ft.com/content/18b3d51d-1e4b-4189-bae2-c31248b6526b.

Williams, Curtis, US Was Top LNG Exporter in 2023 As Hit Record Levels, Reuters, 3 January 2024, https://www.reuters.com/business/energy/us-was-top-lng-exporter-2023-hit-record-levels-2024-01-02/.

Wong, Edward, U.S. and Allies Sound Alarm Over Their Adversaries' Military Ties, New York Times, 30 September 2024, https://www.nytimes.com/2024/09/30/us/politics/us-axis-china-iran-russia.html?tpcc=china_brief&utm_source=Sailthru&utm_medium=email&utm_campaign=China%20Brief%2010012024&utm_term=china_brief.

Wilson, Tom, Russia's Planned Gas Pipeline to China Hit by Construction Delay, Financial Times, 28 January 2024, https://www.ft.com/content/f37f4b84-0d2c-4e7b-882c-3fb26822bb9c.

World Bank, Belt and Road Economics: Opportunities and Risks of Transport Corridors, 18 June 2019, https://www.worldbank.org/en/topic/regional-integration/publication/belt-and-road-economics-opportunities-and-risks-of-transport-corridors.

World Bank, World Bank Group Releases FY22 Audited Financial Statements, 8 August 2022, https://www.worldbank.org/en/news/press-release/2022/08/08/world-bank-group-releases-fy22-audited-financial-statements#:~:text=IBRD's loan portfolio increased to $227.1 billion%2C, well above the prudential minimum liquidity level.

Zalaznick, Matt, How Will the 2020 Biden-Trump Election Impact K-12?, District Administration, 20 October 2020, https://districtadministration.com/article/how-will-the-2020-biden-trump-election-impact-k-12/.

Zhou, Laura, and Orange Wang, How 'Made in China 2025' Became a Lightning Rod in 'War over China's National Destiny', South China Morning Post, 18 January 2019, https://www.scmp.com/news/china/diplomacy/article/2182441/how-made-china-2025-became-lightning-rod-war-over-chinas.

Zion, Ilan Ben, Ex-Israeli Spy Chief: Netanyahu Planned Iran Strike in 2011, Associated Press, 31 May 2018, https://apnews.com/general-news-ff3d8d27040e45f0a24beab254a63e3d.

Zitner, Aaron and Xavier Martinez, Voters Want MAGA Lite From Trump, WSJ Poll Finds, Wall Street Journal, 17 January 2025, https://www.wsj.com/politics/policy/donald-trump-policy-approval-poll-849feb84?page=1.